PRONOUNCING
WELSH PLACE-NAMES

Pronouncing
Welsh Place-names

Tony Leaver

ISBN: 978-1-84527-205-0

Cover design: Alan Jones

First published in 1998 by Gwasg Carreg Gwalch,
12 Iard yr Orsaf, Llanrwst, Wales LL26 0EH
☎ (01492) 642031
Printed and published in Wales.

Contents

Introduction

If you're a visitor to Wales or you've recently come to live here, and you need to ask the way to somewhere, it can be a bit of a challenge. It's fine if you want to go to a place with a straightforward short name like Bangor or Corwen, but if you're heading for Rhosllannerchrugog, Llwyngwril or Llanrhaeadr-ym-Mochnant, you may be tempted to admit defeat and just point at the mind-bending string of letters in the guidebook.

It would be very satisfying, wouldn't it, to be able to reel off Troedrhiwdalar or Pontrhydfendigaid as easily as Birmingham or Newcastle? But most people are put off from even trying because they get the impression that the pronunciation of names like these must be very difficult, or even impossible, if you're not Welsh. They look at Betws-y-coed, for example, and can't work out what to do with the "w", so they just leave it out and end up, as often as not, with that well-known Welsh schoolgirl, Betsy Co-Ed. Some of the Welsh used to believe they had longer tongues than the English, so they could pronounce words that the English couldn't, and when you're faced with something like Eglwyswrw or Llanuwchllyn, you could be forgiven for thinking they might have been right.

So let's get one thing clear straight away. The idea that Welsh pronunciation is difficult is *complete nonsense*.

Admittedly, if you wanted to acquire a perfect Welsh accent, you'd have to be prepared for a bit of study and practice, as with any language. And if you're a visitor, especially if you're on holiday, you've almost certainly got more interesting things to do than sit for hours poring over a textbook. But what if you could manage, *with very little effort*, to get quite a lot of Welsh place names completely right, and almost all the others near enough right so that the Welsh people you meet will know which place you're talking about? This book will show you how to do that.

Your easiest option is the list of Instant Welsh Place Names at the back of the book. It contains most of the well-known Welsh place names and quite a few not so well known. After each name in this list you'll find the pronunciation written out as near as it can be in English spelling. For example, the pronunciation of Ystradgynlais is given as *usstradd-gun-lice*. If you read this off just as if it was a string of English words, you'll have almost exactly the correct Welsh sound of the name. In some cases the English spelling will be close to the correct Welsh sound but slightly off beam in places, as with *mack-unth-leth* for Machynlleth.

But you won't find in this list all the Welsh words you might want to pronounce, and the list won't help you to recognise these words when other people say them. So the rest of the book is designed to introduce you to Welsh pronunciation in general. And you'll be surprised how easy it is.

Welsh spelling, unlike English spelling, is extremely tidy and regular and the rules are mostly very simple and logical. Once you know the rules, you can pronounce almost any Welsh word correctly on sight. And most of the sounds you find in Welsh words are the same, or as near as makes no difference, as sounds we have in English.

Take our old friend Betws-y-coed. The trick here is to know that the "w" is pronounced like an English "oo". If you say *bettooss a koid*, sounding it just as if it was a string of English words, then you'll have almost exactly the correct Welsh pronunciation. There's nothing there that needs a longer than average tongue, and there's nothing there that breaks the standard Welsh spelling rules.

It's true, of course, that there are a few difficult sounds in Welsh names – the famous "ll", for example – but there's no law that says you have to get them 100% right. People who weren't brought up to speak English often have trouble with "th" and say things like "What eez zeess?" for "What is this?", but that doesn't stop English people from understanding them. In this book you'll have the option of either learning these hard sounds or finding ways of fudging them – it's up to you.

So why not have a go? You never know, you might surprise yourself next time you're doing a commentary on your holiday video of Penrhyndeudraeth.

How this book works – Instant Welsh

The first thing to do if you don't know how to pronounce a Welsh place name is to look it up in the Alphabetical List of Instant Welsh Place Names at page 102. Against each name is the sound of that name written as near as possible in English spelling. These English spellings are in *italics*. So for Maentwrog you would have *mine-toorrogg*.

If the name you want isn't in this list, the next thing to do is to look up the first part of the name in the Alphabetical List of Place Name Elements on page 119. This gives all the common Welsh words that are found as part of a place name, and it works the same way as the list of names, except that the meaning is given as well. The **Welsh** spelling will be in **heavy type**. So you'll get things like:

| **llyn** | lake | *thlinn* |
| (Welsh spelling) | (meaning) | (Sound in English spelling) |

If you find the first part of the name in this list, then look up the next part of the name in the same list, and so on until you get to the end of the name. Then you know how to say all the bits of the name, and all you have to do is put them together. It helps to say the whole thing fairly fast, so you may need to run through it a few times for practice.

But it's possible that not all the bits of the name will be in the list, and then you're stuck.

That's where the main part of the book comes in. It aims to make you independent of these lists by giving you enough understanding of Welsh pronunciation to be able to figure out even the hardest place names for yourself.

The name and element lists will also help you to do this if you just browse through them to get the feel of how different letters and groups of letters sound in Welsh.

Finally, there is an Alphabetical List of People's Names on page 132. This works much the same way as the other lists.

If you decide that you want to stick to using these lists and that you don't want to work through any of the main part of the book, read the note about "Natural Breaks" on page 16.

How this book works – Main Sections

The main part of the book comes in three sections.

Section 1 is called BASICS. This gives all the pronunciation rules you absolutely have to know. If you don't want to go any further after you've finished this section, that's fine – you will still have a pretty good Welsh pronunciation.

Section 2 is called REFINEMENTS. This gives a few extra rules which will make your pronunciation just that little bit more correct.

Section 3 is called THE WORKS. For those who've mastered the first two sections and are still raring to go, this section deals with all the tricky bits of Welsh pronunciation that the first two sections skip over.

* * *

Before you go on to the start of the BASICS section, read the pages headed "An Encouragement" (7) and "A Challenge" (8). Also, if you're American, read the page headed "A note for American readers" (6).

A note for Welsh-speaking readers

(Translation below.)

Go brin y bydd arnoch angen prynu'r llyfr hwn i chi'ch hun! (Anrheg i ffrind di-Gymraeg, o bosib?) Ond efallai eich bod wedi bwrw cip drwyddo a sylwi ei fod yn dysgu ynganiad anghywir rhai synau Cymraeg, ac efallai y teimlwch yn anhapus am hyn.

Anelir y llyfr yn bennaf at bobl sydd yn tueddu i ynganu geiriau Cymraeg fel petaent yn eiriau Saesneg oherwydd bod ganddynt yr argraff y byddai ynganiad Cymraeg yn rhy anodd iddynt. A nod y llyfr yw dangos y gallant yn hawdd iawn gyrraedd ynganiad nad yw'n gwbl gywir, yn sicr, ond sydd yn llawer iawn nes at yr ynganiad cwbl gywir nag un sydd yn seiliedig ar reolau sillafu Saesneg. Y gobaith yw y bydd nifer o bobl yn fodlon rhoi cynnig ar hyn na fyddai'n fodlon ymroddi'r amser a'r ymdrech ychwanegol y byddai eu hangen er mwyn dysgu ynganiad cwbl gywir. A'r gobaith hefyd yw y sbardunir rhai ohonynt i fwrw ymlaen i ddysgu'r ynganiad cwbl gywir. Y mae'r llyfr yn cynnwys gwybodaeth lawn ar gyfer y sawl sy'n dewis cymryd y cam hwn.

You're hardly likely to need to buy this book for yourself! (A present for a non Welsh-speaking friend, possibly?) But you may have glanced through it and noticed that it teaches an incorrect pronunciation of some Welsh sounds, and you may feel unhappy about this.

The book is aimed first and foremost at people who tend to pronounce Welsh words as if they were English words because they have the impression that Welsh pronunciation would be too difficult for them. And the book is intended to show that they can very easily acquire a pronunciation which isn't indeed fully correct, but which is very much closer to the fully correct pronunciation than one based on English spelling rules. The hope is that a number of people will be willing to have a go at this who wouldn't want to commit the extra time and effort needed to learn a fully correct pronunciation. And the hope is also that some of them will be spurred on to learn the fully correct pronunciation. The book contains full information for those who choose to take this step.

A note for American readers

Most of the directions given in this book will work equally well for American or British readers, but in a few cases American readers will find they get on better by doing something slightly different:

"a" and "o":

To an English person the Welsh "a" and "o" sound very much like the "a" and "o" in "pat" and "pot". To an American the Welsh "a" sounds more like the "o" in "pot", whereas the Welsh "o" sounds more like the "o" in "corn". So in this book **Madog** is shown as being pronounced *maddogg*, but for an American it's better to think of it as *moddogg*, with the first "o" as in "pot" and the second as in "corn". Putting it another way, "a" and "o" are roughly what they would be in a Spanish word like "tacos".

"t":

Americans sometimes pronounce "t" so that it sounds exactly like "d". For example, "waiter" can sound just like "wader". This never happens in Welsh (although there was a time about 1,400 years ago when it did). This book shows **Betws** as being pronounced *bettooss*, which an American might tend to pronounce as *beddooss*. The end of this word needs to sound like *-tooss*. *Bett-tooss*, said as two words, is nearer right than *beddooss*.

Sometimes "t" gets left out altogether. "Interesting", for example, can sound like "inneresting". Again, this doesn't happen in Welsh.

"r":

Americans (unless they come from New England) will handle the Welsh "r" much better than English people will. Americans won't need to read the section in THE WORKS on the "correct" pronunciation of "r" – they'll get by just fine with what it says in the REFINEMENTS section.

An Encouragement

Here is a list of some Welsh place names that you can get right, or nearly right, without reading this book at all:

Amroth	Creignant	Nant Gwyn
Arthog	Criggion	Nantmel
Baglan	Dinnant	Pant-glas
Banc Gwyn	Dolgarrog	Parc-gwyn
Bangor	Ffestiniog	Penbontbren
Banwen	Ffinnant	Pencarreg
Beili-brith	Garnant	Penlan
Bodnant	Garnwen	Penmon
Bodran	Garth Heilyn	Pennal
Bolbro	Glaslyn	Pennant
Boncath	Glasnant	Pen-pont
Borth-wen	Glyncornel	Pen-sarn
Bryn-cras	Gorseinon	Pontcanna
Bryn-glas	Gwent	Pontgarreg
Bryn-gwyn	Harlech	Pontrobert
Bryn-teg	Hendra	Powys
Cadnant	Hendy-gwyn	Pren-gwyn
Camlo	Margam	Rheidol
Camnant	Meidrim	Rhyl
Carn Ingli	Meity	Talgarreg
Carno	Migneint	Talgarth
Carreg Wen	Morlan	Tal-sarn
Carrog	Mostyn	Talwen
Colwyn	Nanmor	Tan-lan
Conwy	Nantcol	Ton-teg
Corris	Nant Ffrancon	Torbant
Corwen	Nant-glas	Trefforest

A Challenge

To get you off to a flying start, why not grasp the nettle and have a go at

The Notorious Welsh "LL"

It's not nearly as hard as people imagine, and if you can get it right, it will make your Welsh pronunciation sound really impressive. And if you can't, so what? You can easily fudge it. (See later.)

So here goes:

* Put the **TIP** of your **TONGUE** against the back of your **TOP TEETH**, just where they meet the gum. (The **TTTT** rule.)

* Hold it in that position.

* Blow gently.

And that's it.

Practise it a few times, then see if you can manage to slip it into a few Welsh words like:

Llandeilo
Llandrindod
Llangollen
Llanelli

Remember "ll" has this sound *anywhere* in a Welsh word, not just at the beginning.

Can't do it? Never mind. Just say "thl" instead. (See later.)

Basics

How this section works

This section covers the most important differences between Welsh and English spelling.

Each letter or group of letters that has a different sound in Welsh (such as "f" or "ll") has a page to itself, called a "rule page".

At the top of the page will be the letter or group of letters that the page deals with. If there is a star (*) after it, that means the true Welsh sound of this letter or these letters can't be shown in English spelling and the pronunciation given here is the closest that English spelling can get. There will be more details on how to pronounce the true Welsh sound somewhere else in the book, and there will be a page number where you can look them up if you want to.

After this there will be:

* an example of a Welsh word which has that letter or those letters in it, with its meaning and its pronunciation in English spelling;

* an explanation of the rule, with maybe some comments;

* more examples;

* some Welsh words without the English spelling, so that you can work out how you think they should sound.

At the bottom of a later page (so you don't see it too soon) the English spelling will be given so you can check if you got it right.

The examples will mostly be words you might find as part of a place name, like "field", "hill", "well", "wood" and so on. Otherwise they'll be common ordinary Welsh words. In some cases a less common word had to be chosen because it was easier to pronounce than any of the common ones.

The meaning and pronunciation are shown in the same way as in the list of elements. So, for example, you might get:

coed	wood	*koid*
(Welsh spelling)	(meaning)	(Sound in English spelling)

Important Note: The English spellings in *italics* are meant to be pronounced exactly as if they were English words. If there is an *"ll"* in the English spelling, for example, it's an English *"ll"*, not a Welsh one.

In some cases the English spelling will include real English words. For example, the Welsh word **waun** sounds almost exactly like the English word "wine".

It's best to pronounce the English spellings quite fast, running all the parts into each other. This very often helps to get the right Welsh sound. You might have to have a couple of practice runs first.

* * *

At the end of the section you'll get a chance to practise what you've learnt on complete place names.

a, e, i, o

Example: **Madog**   (person's name)   *maddogg*

Rule: **Pronounce "a", "e", "i", "o" as in "pat", "pet", "pit", "pot".**

* It often helps to imagine that the next letter after the "a","e", "i" or "o" is doubled. For example, the "a" in "scrapping" sounds different from the "a" in "scraping".

More examples:

hebog	hawk	*hebbogg*
dinas	fort, city	*dinnass*
noson	evening	*nossonn*

Now, how would you pronounce these?

caban	hut
Peris	(person's name)
cribin	rake
blodyn	flower

See bottom of page 15 for suggested answers.

ae, ai

Example: **maen**   stone   *mine*

Rule: **Pronounce "ae" and "ai" as "eye".**

* * These sound just like the English word "eye".

More examples:

cae	field	*kye*
plaid	party	*plide*
traeth	beach	*trye-th*
craig	rock	*krye-g*

(*krye-g* rhymes with the first part of "tig-er".)

Now, how would you pronounce these?

blaen	summit
brain	crows
saint	saints

See bottom of page 19 for suggested answers.

aw

Example: **cawl**   soup   *cowl*

Rule: Pronounce "aw" as "ow".

* This is "ow" as in "now", **not** as in "low".

More examples:

brawd	brother	*browd*
Awst	August	*oust*

Now, how would you pronounce these?

hawl	claim
naw	nine
dawn	talent

See bottom of page 20 for suggested answers.

Answers from page 13 - *cabbann, perriss, cribbinn, bloddinn.*

Natural Breaks

Mixed in among the rules you'll find "Natural Break" pages like this next one. These pages deal with various topics connected with Welsh pronunciation. There's nothing on these pages that you have to learn in order to be able to pronounce Welsh place names. But you'll get on better if you don't skip them. They're there to give you a rest from the rules and to give what you've been reading a chance to sink in.

The best of all is if you take a proper break (half an hour, an hour, several hours, a day) after each of the Natural Breaks. If you can manage in this way to spread each of the main sections over several days, doing only a few minutes each day, that gives you the best possible chance of remembering the rules you've learnt - because the last rule you looked at won't be so easily driven out of your mind by the next one before it's had time to bed down in your memory.

You can also dip into the Natural Break pages any time you want, even if you're not doing (and perhaps not intending to do) the section they come in. Each Natural Break page is complete in itself, and you don't have to have read any other part of the book to be able to make sense of it.

Common Welsh Phrases

If you're talking to somebody who speaks Welsh (for example, if you're ordering a drink in a cafe or pub), it's nice to be able to show that you've taken the trouble to pick up a few phrases of the language. Try these:

Hello	**S'mae**	*smye*
Can I have...	**Ga' i...**	*guy...*
Can we have...	**Gawn ni...**	*gowny...* (rhymes with "towny")
...a tea?	**...de?**	*...day*
...two teas?	**...ddau de?**	*...thy day*
...a coffee?	**...goffi?**	*...goffee*
...two coffees?	**...ddau goffi**	*...thy goffee*
...a coffee and a tea?	**...goffi a the?**	*...goffee ath ay*
...a beer?	**...gwrw?**	*...guru*
...two beers?	**...ddau gwrw?**	*...thy guru*
...milk?	**...laeth?**	*...lye-th*
...sugar?	**...siwgr?**	*...shooggoor*
Please	**Plîs**	*please*
Excuse me	**Esgusodwch fi**	*essky-soddook vee*
Sorry	**Mae'n flin 'da fi**	*mine vleen davvy*
I don't understand	**Dwi ddim yn dallt**	*dooey thimm un dath-t*
Thanks very much	**Diolch yn fawr**	*dee-olk unn vowr* (rhymes with "hour")
No thanks	**Dim diolch**	*dim dee-olk*
Goodbye	**Hwyl**	*who-ill*

And you might hear some of these in reply:

Beth hoffech chi?	What would you like?	*bairth hoffeck-ee*
Cewch	Yes you can	*kayook*
Wrth gwrs	Of course	*oorth goorss*

Take a Break!

c, ch*

Example: **cist**   box   *kist*

Rule: Pronounce "c" and "ch" as "k".

* "c" in Welsh **never** sounds like "s", as in "cell".
* For more information about "ch", see page 81.

More examples:

cennin	leek	*kenninn*
cylch	circle	*kilk*
napcyn	napkin	*napkin*
chwilen	beetle	*quillenn*

Now, how would you pronounce these?

cil	corner
cerrig	stones
poncyn	hillock
chwip	whip

See bottom of page 21 for suggested answers.

Answers from page 14 - *bline, brine, sign-t.*

dd*

Example: **ddim**   nothing   *thimm*

Rule: Pronounce "dd" as "th".

* This applies to "dd" **anywhere in a word**, not just at the beginning.
* For more information about "dd", see page 82.

More examples:

meddyg	doctor	*meth-igg*
nentydd	brooks	*nenn-tith*
ganddynt	with them	*gann-thint*
ddringon	climbed	*thring-onn*

Now, how would you pronounce these?

ddant	tooth
pontydd	bridges
toddi	melt

See bottom of page 24 for suggested answers.

Answers from page 15 - *howl, now, down.*

f, ff

Example: **Cadfan**   (person's name)   *kadd-vann*

Rule: Pronounce "f" as "v".

  *   But pronounce "ff" as in English.

Examples:

fam	mother	*vamm*
fryn	hill	*vrinn*
canrif	century	*cann-rivv*

But: **ffrog**   frock   *frogg*

Now, how would you pronounce these?

fanc	bank
pentref	village
ffilm	film

See bottom of page 25 for suggested answers.

Answers from page 19 - *kill, kerrigg, ponn-kinn, quip*

ThatplaceinWaleswiththelongname...

Learn how to say it and astonish your friends!

Here it is - it only just fits on one line:

Llanfairpwllgwyngyllgogerychwyrndrobwllllantysiliogogogoch

Now, let's take it slowly:

llan	church	*thlann*
fair	Mary	*vyre*
pwll	pool	*pooth*
gwyn	white	*gwinn*
gyll	hazel	*gith*
goger y	near the	*gogg-erra*
chwyrn	rapid	*kweern*
drobwll	whirlpool	*drobbooth*
llan	church	*lann*
tysilio	(saint's name)	*tuss-ill-yo*
gogo	cave	*goggo*
goch	red	*gauk*

Nowpractisetillyoucansayitwithoutstumblinginthreeseconds!

But please, please, don't take it too seriously! The real name of this village in Anglesey is Llanfair Pwllgwyngyll. Someone lengthened it for a joke in the 19th century, hoping it would attract the tourists.

Take a Break!

g

Example: **gest**   belly   *guest* (not *jest*)

Rule: Pronounce "g" as in "get".

* "g" in Welsh **never** sounds like "j", as in "gentle".

More examples:

cragen	shell	*kraggenn*
gini	guinea	*guinea*
gig	meat	*gig* (not *jig*)

Now, how would you pronounce these?

gil	corner
bargen	bargain
cregyn	shells

See bottom of page 26 for suggested answers.

Answers from page 20 - *thant, ponn-tith, tothy* ("oth" as in "bother")

ll*

Example: **llan**   church   *thlann*

Rule: Pronounce "ll" as "thl".

* This applies to "ll" **anywhere in a word**, not just at the beginning.
* If you can't manage "thl" comfortably in a particular word, just say "th".
* For more information about "ll", see page 8.

More examples:

dillad	clothes	*dith-ladd*
allt	hillside	*ath-t*
pistyll	waterfall	*pistith*

Now, how would you pronounce these?

llyn	lake
collen	hazel
castell	castle

See bottom of page 29 for suggested answers.

Answers from page 21 - *vank, penn-trevv, film.*

oe

Example: **coed**   wood   *koid*

Rule: Pronounce "oe" as "oi".

More examples:

croen	skin	*kroin*
oed	age	*oid*

Now, how would you pronounce these?

moel	bare hill
poeth	hot

See bottom of page 30 for suggested answers.

Answers from page 24 - *ghyll* (not *jill*), *barg-enn* (not *barge-enn*), *kregginn*.

A Few Welsh Words...

... that you might have seen in books or newspapers, or that you might see around you on your travels through Wales. Maybe you already know what they mean - some of them, anyway - but do you know how to say them? (In the right-hand column "ah" is to be pronounced as "ah!" where marked with a star.)

ar werth	for sale	*ar wairth*
bara brith	currant bread	*barrah* breeth*
Blas ar Gymru	Taste of Wales	*blahss* ar gumm-ry*
CADW	ancient monuments organisation	*kaddoo*
cawl cennin	leek soup	*cowl kenninn*
Croeso i Gymru	Welcome to Wales	*kroisso ee gumm-ry*
cwm	mountain valley	*koomm*
Dynion	Gentlemen	*dunn-yonn*
Eisteddfod(au)	cultural festival(s)	*aiss-teth-vodd-(eye)*
Eryri	Snowdonia	*errurry*
Gorsedd	cultural celebrities who run the Eisteddfod	*gorseth*
gwyniad	whiting	*gwinn-yadd*
hiraeth	nostalgia	*hear-eye-th*
hwyl	religious fervour	*hooill*
Iechyd da!	Good health!	*yecky dah!**
Llwybr Cyhoeddus	Public Footpath	*thlooibbeer k-ahoy-this*
Mabinogion	collection of ancient stories	*mabby-nogg-yonn*
Meibion Glyndwr	anti-English activists	*maib-yonn glinn-dooer*
Merched	Ladies	*mair-kedd*
Plaid Cymru	Welsh National Party	*plide kumm-ry*
Pobol y Cwm	soap opera	*pobboll a koomm*
Radio Cymru	Welsh radio	*radd-yo kumm-ry*
S4C	Welsh TV	*ess pedd-wah* reck*
Tylwyth Teg	fairies	*tull-ooith taig*

Take a Break!

u

Example: **pump**   five   as if **pimp**   *pimp*

Rule: Pronounce "u" as Welsh "i".

* Wherever you see "u" in a word, imagine that it's "i" and pronounce the word as if it was.

More examples:

munud	minute	as if **minid**	*minnidd*
Curig	(person's name)	as if **Cirig**	*kirrig*
waun	moor	as if **wain**	*wine*
beudy	cowshed	as if **beidy**	*baidy*

Now, how would you pronounce these?

Tudno	(person's name)
dau	two
deu	two

See bottom of page 31 for suggested answers.

Answers from page 25 - *thlinn, koth-lenn, kass-teth.*

29

w*

Example: **twlc**   pigsty   *toolk*

Rule: Pronounce "w" as "oo".

* This only applies to words where you can't easily manage to pronounce it the normal English way.
* For more information about "w", see pages 72, 93, 96.

Examples:

crwn	round	*kroonn*
cwrt	court	*kooert*
eglwys	church	*egg-lewis*
Wrw	(person's name)	*oorroo*

But:

gwyn	white	*gwinn*

Now, how would you pronounce these?

cwm	valley
gwr	man
brwyn	rushes
wen	white

See bottom of page 34 for suggested answers.

Answers from page 26 - *moil, poith.*

y

Example: **ynys**   island   *unniss*

Rule: Pronounce "y" as "u" in "cut".

* * Near the end of a word "y" sounds just like a Welsh "i".
* * But you can pronounce the little words **y**, **ym**, **yn**, **yng** and **yr** as *uh*, *umm*, *unn*, *ung* and *urr*.
* * As with "a", "e", "i" and "o", it often helps to imagine that the next letter after the "y" is doubled.

More examples:

ffynnon   well   *funnonn*

But:

bryn (as if **brin**)   hill   *brinn*
popty (as if **popti**)   oven   *popp-ty*
Dol-y-Bont   (place name)   *doll-a-bont*

Now, how would you pronounce these?

ystrad   valley
dyffryn   valley
pandy   fulling mill
Pen-y-Bryn   (place name)

See bottom of page 35 for suggested answers.

Answers from page 29 - *tidd-no*, *die*, *day*.

English Words in Welsh

When people are speaking Welsh they often use English words. Sometimes they do it just for a laugh, but also there are quite a lot of English words that have become part of the Welsh language by now.

Because Welsh spelling is so tidy, they don't like to spoil it by bringing in words in English spelling, so they change the spelling to fit the Welsh rules. The results can look very odd to someone who doesn't speak Welsh.

See how many of these English words you can recognise in their Welsh disguise. Some are very easy, some are quite hard. If you get stuck, go to page 39.

banc	bargen	bathrwm
bil	bocs	bun
bwci	bwletin	carnifal
cloc	coci	coffi
fat	festri	ffacs
ffactri	ffansi	fferet
fflat	fflyffi	fforc
haia!	hipi	jacet
lefel	lobi	lownj
lyfli	marc	mwnci
parc	piti	platfform
pwdin	refferendwm	roc
rygbi	selebriti	sensitif
seremoni	sgôr	sgowt
sigarét	sinema	sisi
sustem	syrcas	tacl
tenis	trebl	tships

Take a Break!

Place Name Practice - 1

Now that you've learnt the basic rules, here are some easy examples of complete place names with their pronunciation in English spelling. If you're not sure why the pronunciation is what it is, the right hand column shows which letters in the word are likely to be a problem and gives you the page numbers where the rules for these letters can be found.

Basaleg	*bass-allegg*	a/e 13
Cilmeri	*kill-merry*	c 19 e/i 13
Clwyd	*klooidd*	w 30
Clynnog	*klunnogg*	o 13 y 31
Llanboidy	*thlann-boidy*	ll 25
Nanhoron	*nann-horronn*	o 13
Teifi	*tavy*	f 21
Tregaron	*tregg-arronn*	a/e/o 13

Now here are some for you to try yourself. Again, the letters that could be a problem are shown in the right hand column, together with the page numbers where the rules for those letters are. But have a go at pronouncing the name before you look up the rule pages.

Elan	a/e 13
Llyn Ogwen	e 13 ll 25
Nant Peris	e 13
Pen-y-bryn	y 31
Porthmadog	a/o 13
Prestatyn	a/e 13
Tanat	a 13
Tremadog	a/e/o 13

Suggested pronunciation for these is on page 37.

Answers from page 30 - *koomm, gooer, bruin* (rhymes with "ruin"), *wen*.

Place Name Practice - 2

These ones are a little bit harder, with more problem letters.

Aberaeron	*abbair-eye-ronn*	a/e/o 13 ae 14
Afon-wen	*avvonn-wenn*	a/e/o 13 f 21
Amlwch	*amm-look*	ch 19 w 30
Bagillt	*baggith-t*	a 13 g 24 ll 25
Crymych	*krummick*	ch 19 y 31
Cwmystwyth	*koomm-uss-tooith*	w 30 y 31
Llanbadarn	*thlann-baddarn*	a 13 ll 25
Llanelli	*thlann-ethly*	a 13 ll 25
Llangadfan	*thlann-gadd-vann*	a 13 f 21 ll 25
Moel Hebog	*moil hebbogg*	e/o 13 oe 26
Pentrefelin	*penn-trevv-ellin*	e 13 f 21
Pen y Fan	*penn-a-vann*	f 21 y 31
Porthdinllaen	*porth-dinn-thline*	ae 14 ll 25
Scethrog	*sketh-rogg*	c 19 o 13

Now some for you to try. Again, have a go before you look up the rule pages.

Cenarth	c 19 e 13
Llanarmon	a/o 13 ll 25
Llanelltud	a 13 ll 25
Llangefni	f 21 ll 25
Llangollen	e 13 ll 25
Llangrannog	o 13 ll 25
Llanrwst	ll 25 w 30
Llantrisant	a/i 13 ll 25
Menai	ai 14 e 13
Nefyn	e 13 f 21
Tal-y-bont	a 13 y 31

Suggested pronunciation on page 37.

Answers from page 31 - *uss-tradd, duff-rinn, pann-dy, penn-a-brinn.*

Place Name Practice - 3

The real heavy stuff.

Bancycapel	*bank-a-kappell*	a/e 13 c 19 y 31
Bylchau	*bulk-eye*	ai 14 ch 19 u 29 y 31
Capel Curig	*kappell kirrigg*	a/e/i 13 c 19 u 29
Carnedd Dafydd	*karneth davvith*	a/e 13 dd 20 f 21
Dolgellau	*dolg-ethl-eye*	ai 14 ll 25 u 29
Llanaelhaearn	*thlann-isle-high-arn*	a 13 ae 14 ll 25
Llechwedd	*thleck-weth*	ch 19 dd 20 ll 25
Machynlleth	*mack-unth-leth*	a 13 ch 19 ll 25 y 31
Mawddach	*mouthe-ack*	aw 15 ch 19 dd 20
Pwllheli	*pooth-helly*	e 13 ll 25 w 30
Tonyrefail	*tonn-a-revvile*	ai 14 e/o 13 f 21 y 31
		(rhymes with "smile")

Your turn now. No help this time - you're on your own.

> Bancyfelin
> Betws-y-coed
> Dan-y-graig
> Llangurig
> Llanllyfni
> Llanwddin
> Maenclochog
> Maentwrog
> Rhuddlan
> Tal-y-llyn

Suggested pronunciation on page 38.

Place Name Practice - Answers

From page 34:

Elan	*ellann*	a/e 13
Llyn Ogwen	*thlinn ogg-wenn*	e 13 ll 25
Nant Peris	*nant perriss*	e 13
Pen-y-bryn	*penn-a-brinn*	y 31
Porthmadog	*porth-maddogg*	a/o 13
Prestatyn	*press-tattinn*	a/e 13
Tanat	*tannatt*	a 13
Tremadog	*tremm-addogg*	a/e/o 13

From page 35:

Cenarth	*kenn-arth*	c 19 e 13
Llanarmon	*thlann-armonn*	a/o 13 ll 25
Llanelltud	*thlann-eth-tidd*	ll 25
Llangefni	*thlann-gevv-ny*	f 21 ll 25
Llangollen	*thlann-goth-lenn*	e 13 ll 25
Llangrannog	*thlann-grannogg*	o 13 ll 25
Llanrwst	*thlann-roost*	ll 25 w 30
Llantrisant	*thlann-trissant*	a/i 13 ll 25
Menai	*menn-eye*	ai 14 e 13
Nefyn	*nevvinn*	e 13 f 21
Tal-y-bont	*tal-a-bont*	a 13 y 31
	("tal" rhymes with "pal")	

Place Name Practice - Answers

From page 36:

Bancyfelin	*bank-a-vellinn*	a/e 13 c 19 f 21 y 31
Betws-y-coed	*bettooss-a-koid*	e 13 oe 26 w 30 y 31
Dan-y-graig	*danna-grye-g*	a 13 ai 14 y 31
Llangurig	*thlann-girrigg*	g 24 i 13 ll 25 u 29
	("g" as in "give")	
Llanllyfni	*thlann-thluvv-ny*	f 21 ll 25 y 31
Llanwddin	*thlann-oothe-inn*	a 13 dd 20 w 30
Maenclochog	*mine-klockogg*	ae 14 ch 19 o 13
Maentwrog	*mine-toorrogg*	ae 14 o 13 w 30
Rhuddlan	*rith-lann*	a 13 dd 20 u 29
Tal-y-llyn	*tal-a-thlinn*	a 13 ll 25 y 31
	("tal" rhymes with "pal")	

End of BASICS Section

If the answers on the last two pages weren't too much of a surprise to you, that means you've picked up a pretty good basic Welsh pronunciation. Congratulations! Have a cup of tea, or if you prefer, a pint of Felinfoel (you should know how to say that by now) or something similar to celebrate - you've earned it. Then have a rest. Then have a go at the next section. It works much the same way as this one, and you won't have any trouble with it.

If you still don't feel too sure, have the cup of tea or the pint of Felinfoel (*vellinn-voil*) and the rest anyway, then have a quick run through the rules and the place name practice again. It'll probably click this time.

English Words in Welsh

Answers from page 32:

bank	bargain	bathroom
bill	box	bin
bookie	bulletin	carnival
clock	cocky	coffee
vat	vestry	fax
factory	fancy	ferret
flat	fluffy	fork
hiya!	hippy	jacket
level	lobby	lounge
lovely	mark	monkey
park	pity	platform
pudding	referendum	rock
rugby	celebrity	sensitive
ceremony	score	scout
cigarette	cinema	cissy
system	circus	tackle
tennis	treble	chips

REFINEMENTS

aer, air, aur*

Example: **caer**   fort   *kyre*

Rule: Pronounce "aer/air/aur" as "ire".

* * These sound almost like the English word "ire".
* * For more information about "r", see page 87.

More examples:

Mair	Mary	*mire*
pair	cauldron	*pyre*
aur	gold	*ire*

Now, how would you pronounce these?

aer	air
gair	word
tair	three

See bottom of page 43 for suggested answers.

awr*

Example: **awr**   hour   *our*

Rule: Pronounce "awr" as "our".

* This sounds almost like the English word "our".
* For more information about "r", see page 87.

More examples:

nawr	now	*nowr*
clawr	book cover	*clowr*
lawr	down	*lowr*

These all rhyme with "hour".

Now, how would you pronounce these?

mawr	great
cawr	giant

See bottom of page 44 for suggested answers.

-e*

Example: **pentre**   village   *penn-tray*

Rule: Pronounce final "e" as "ay".

* This is the sound of "e" at the end of a word. In English "e" at the end of a word is usually not sounded at all, so "grate" sounds just like "great".
* For more information about "-e", see page 93.

More examples:

tre	town	*tray*
Hepste	(river name)	*hepp-stay*
de	right, south	*day*

Now, how would you pronounce these?

te	tea
hendre	winter home
le	place

See bottom of page 45 for suggested answers.

Answers from page 41 - *ire, ghyre* ("gh" as in "ghost"), *tyre*.

-ed, -es

Examples: **carped** carpet *kar-pedd*
           proffes profession *proffess*

Rule: **Pronounce "-ed/-es" as "edd/ess".**

* This is the sound of "ed" or "es" at the end of a word. In English the "e" is usually not sounded, so "seemed" sounds like "seemd".
* This fits with the "double the next letter" rule (page 13).

More examples:

parthed about *par-thedd*
santes female saint *sann-tess*

Now, how would you pronounce these?

toiled toilet
arthes she-bear

See bottom of page 48 for suggested answers.

Answers from page 42 - *mowr, kowr* (both rhyme with "hour")

44

ei, eu*

Examples: **Einon**   (person's name)   *ainonn*
           euog   guilty   *ayogg*

Rule: Pronounce "ei/eu" as "ai".

* For more information about "ei/eu", see page 84.

More examples:

Rheidol	(river name)	*ray-doll*
beudy	cowshed	*baidy*
deu	two	*day*

Now, how would you pronounce these?

eithin	gorse
beili	yard
heulog	sunny

See bottom of page 49 for suggested answers.

Answers from page 43 - *tay, henn-dray, lay*

More Common Welsh Phrases

Phrases that you can use in a cafe, pub or shop, or on various occasions. Remember "ah" is as in "ah!" (marked with a "*").

Can I have ...	Ga' i ...	*guy ...*
... this?	... hwn?	*... hoon*
... one of these?	... un o'r rhain?	*... eenor ine*

How much is it?	Faint ydy o?	*vine tuddy o*
How much are they?	Faint ydan nhw?	*vine tudda noo*
... each?	... 'r un?	*... er een*
In English	Yn Saesneg	*un suss-naig*

I'd like	Mi hoffwn i ...	*mee hoffoonn ee*
... a piece of cake	... ddarn o deisen	*tharn o daissenn*
... a sandwich	... frechdan	*vreck-dann*
... a pint of beer	... beint o gwrw	*baint o guru*
... half a pint	... hanner peint	*hannair paint*
... an orange juice	...sudd oren	*seethe orrenn*

| Where's the loo? | Lle mae'r ty bach? | *thlay mire tee bahk*|

| Great! | Gwych! | *gweek* |
| Cheers! | Iechyd da! | *yecky dah*|

How are you?	Sut dach chi?	*siddack ee*
Very well	Da iawn	*dah* yown*
	(rhymes with "gown")	
And you?	A chi?	*ah* kee*

Phrases you might hear:

Rhywbeth arall?	Anything else?	*roobeth arrath*
Ga' i helpu?	Can I help?	*guy helpy*
Ga' i'ch helpu chi?	Can I help you?	*gike helpy kee*
Iawn	OK	*yown*
		(rhymes with "gown")

Take a Break!

er*

Example: **gwern**   swamp   *gwairn*

Rule: Pronounce "er" as "air".

* This is **only** when you find yourself wanting to pronounce it like "ur" (as in the English word "her").
  In any other case "e" sounds as in "pet" (page 13).
* For more information about "r", see page 87.

More examples:

sgert	skirt	*skairt*
fferm	farm	*fairm*
berwi	boil	*bairwy*

But:

Peris	(person's name)	*perriss*

Now, how would you pronounce these?

perth	hedge, bush
term	term
derbyn	receive

See bottom of page 50 for suggested answers.

Answers from page 44 - *toiledd, ar-thess*

ia, ie, io

Example: **Iestyn**   (person's name)   *yess-tinn*

Rule: Pronounce "i" as "y" before "a/e/o".

* So pronounce "ia" as "ya", "iai" as "yai", "iaw" as "yaw", "ie" as "ye", "iei" as "yei", "io" as "yo" etc.
* The "a", "ai", "aw", "e" and "o" should still be pronounced as explained earlier.

More examples:

iard	yard	*yard*
teithion	travelled	*taith-yonn*
ieir	hens	*yair*
iawn	all right	*yown* (rhymes with "gown")

Now, how would you pronounce these?

iâr	hen
meibion	sons
iet	gate

See bottom of page 51 for suggested answers.

Answers from page 45 - *aithinn, bailey, hailogg*

ir, ur*

Examples: **tir**   land   *teer*
             mur   wall   *mere*

Rule: Pronounce "ir" and "ur" as "ear".

* "ir" and "ur" sound just like the English word "ear".
* This is **only** when you find yourself wanting to pronounce them like "er" (as in the English words "stir" and "fur"). In any other case "i" sounds as in "pit" (page 13) and "u" sounds the same as "i" (page 29).
* For more information about "r", see page 87.

More examples:

pentir   headland   *penn-teer*
eglur   clear   *egg-lear*

but:

Curig   (saint's name)   *kirrigg*

Now, how would you pronounce these?

sir   county
pur   pure
antur   adventure

See bottom of page 52 for suggested answers.

Answers from page 48 - *pairth, tairm, dair-binn.*

iw, uw*

Examples: **miw**   mew   *mew*

                   uwd   porridge   *ewd*

Rule: Pronounce "iw" as "ew".

* In some words "ew" is hard to say - just say "oo".

* Pronounce "uw" just like "iw".

* For more information about "iw", see page 85.

More examples:

tiwb	tube	*tube*
sgriw	screw	*screw*
Huw	Hugh	*hugh*

Now, how would you pronounce these?

criw	crew
niwl	mist
Puw	Pugh

See bottom of page 55 for suggested answers.

Answers from page 49 - *yar, maib-yonn, yett*

S

Example: **cors**   bog   *coarse/course*

Rule: Pronounce "s" as "ss".

* Welsh "s" never sounds like "z", as in "rose".
* "s" and "h" are usually kept separate. **Ynyshir** is *unniss-hear*, not *unny-shear*.

More examples:

teisen	cake	*tay-senn*
hosan	sock	*hossann*
Seisnig	English	*saiss-nigg*

Now, how would you pronounce these?

noson	evening
commins	common

See bottom of page 56 for suggested answers.

Answers from page 50 - *seer, peer, ann-teer.*

Road Signs

No problem when the English version is uppermost, but what about when it's the Welsh version?

Don't waste vital moments - learn what they mean and how they sound, so you can read them just as fast as if they were in English.

allanfa	exit	*athlann-vah** ("ah!")
anaddas	unsuitable	*ann-athass*
arafwch	slow down	*aravv-ook*
arhoswch	stop, wait	*ar-hossook*
canol y dref	town centre	*kannoll a dray*
di-dâl	free	*dee-dah*-l*
dim cerbydau	no vehicles	*dimm kair-budd-eye*
dim marciau	no markings	*dimm marky-eye*
dim mynediad	no entry	*dimm munnedd-yadd*
dim parcio	no parking	*dimm park-yo*
diwedd	end	*dee-weth*
ewch i'ch lôn	get in lane	*ayook ick lawn*
ffordd ar gau	road closed	*forth arg eye*
gwasanaethau	services	*gwassann-eye-thigh*
gwyriad	diversion	*gweery-add*
ildiwch	give way	*ild-yook*
llath	yard(s)	*thlah*-th*
milltir	mile(s)	*mith-teer*
mynedfa	entrance	*munnedd-vah**
maes parcio	car park	*mice park-yo*
pob cerbyd	all vehicles	*paub kair-bidd*
rheolaeth traffig	traffic control	*ray-oll-eye-th traffigg*
peidiwch ...	don't ...	*paid-yook*
toiledau	toilets	*toy-ledd-eye*
un rhes	single file	*een race*

Now your quiz questions:

What's the Welsh for "no ... "?
And what three letters on the end of a word indicate that it's telling you to do or not to do something?

Take a Break!

si

Example: **siop**   shop   *shop*

Rule: Pronounce "si" as "sh".

   *   This is **only** when the next letter is "a", "e", "o", "w" or "y".

More examples:

siec	cheque	*sheck*
siart	chart	*shart*
teision	stacked	*tay-shonn*

Now, how would you pronounce these?

sioc	shock
sied	shed
pinsion	pinch

See bottom of page 57 for suggested answers.

Answers from page 51 - *crew, newl, pew.*

wr*

Example: **cwrt**   court   *kooert*

Rule: Pronounce "wr" as "ooer".

* This is almost the same sound as the end of the word "brewer", but said quickly.
* For more information about "r", see page 87.

More examples:

tŵr	tower	*tooer*
wrth	by	*ooerth*
dwrn	fist	*dooern*

Now, how would you pronounce these?

dŵr	water
swrth	drowsy

See bottom of page 58 for suggested answers.

Answers from page 52 - *nossonn, kommince*

56

yr*

Example: **byr**   short   *beer*

Rule: Pronounce "yr" as "ear".

* "yr" sounds almost like the English word "ear".
* This is **only** when "yr" is near the end of a word **and** you find yourself wanting to pronounce it like "ur" (as in the English word "myrtle"). Near the beginning of a word, if you feel like pronouncing it as "ur", you can. Otherwise see page 31.
* For more information about "r", see page 87.

More examples:

syrth	substance	*seerth*
teimlyr	tentacle	*taim-leer*

But:

syrcas	circus	*sur-kass*

Now, how would you pronounce these?

tyrd	come
gwesgyr	spreads
dyrnod	blow

See bottom of page 61 for suggested answers.

Answers from page 55 - *shock, shed, pinn-shon*

yw*

Example: **Tywyn**   (place name)   *toe-inn*

Rule: Pronounce "yw" as "oe".

* But near the end of a word pronounce "yw" like the English word "you".
* And if "you" won't work, just say "oo".
* For more information about "yw", see page 85.

More examples:

ywen	yew tree	*owe-enn*

But:

byw	live	*bew*
distryw	destruction	*diss-troo*

Now, how would you pronounce these?

tywod	sand
yw	is
brithryw	all kinds

See bottom of page 62 for suggested answers.

Answers from page 56 - *dooer, sooerth*.

More English Words in Welsh

Again, some of these are very easy, some are quite hard. Also some of them are a bit different from the ones you've had before. These are ones where the Welsh word doesn't sound quite the same as the English word, or the rules of Welsh spelling have had to be bent a bit to cope with the English word. Have fun! Answers on page 66.

ambiwlans	balans	bambŵ
beic	brêc	bysus
clir	cês	coctêl
cownsul	cŵl	cyrtans
ddy mŵfi	dêt	dôl
dowt	ecspres	eniwê
eroplên	ficer	fflêcs
ffliwc	fflydleit	ffortiwn
ffrynt	gêm	grêfi
grêt	grŵp	gyts
hiwmor	interfiw	iot
lein-yp	nêfi blw	neis
nymbar	nyrs	owns
peint	picil	piws
polisi	proses	pync
reis	reit	ryff geid
salŵn	seliwloid	sgersli bilîf
sgrym	sgŵp	siampŵ
sioc	siop	siwgwr
siwr	siwt	slei
sosej	steil	streic
strîc	sybyrb	teils
trên	twnnel	twrist
tyff	wîcend	wncwl

"Têc y Brêc!"

Place Name Practice - 1

A mixture of sounds from BASICS and REFINEMENTS.

Bangor Is-coed	*bang-gor-eess-koid*	**oe** 26 **s** 52
Breidden	*bray-thenn*	**dd** 20 **ei** 45
Claerwen	*klyre-wenn*	**aer** 41 **e** 13
Cricieth	*krick-yeth*	**c** 19 **ie** 49
Fforest Fawr	*forrest vowr*	**awr** 42 **e** 13 **f** 21
	("owr" rhymes with "hour")	
Hirwaun	*heer-wine*	**ai** 14 **i** 13 **ir** 50
Llandeilo	*thlann-dailo*	**ei** 45 **ll** 25
Merthyr	*mair-theer*	**er** 48 **yr** 57
Nant yr Eira	*nant-a-rairah*	**ei** 45 **y** 31,57
	("ah" as in "ah!")	
Ogwr	*oggooer*	**o** 13 **wr** 56
Penrhyndeudraeth	*penn-rinn-day-drye-th*	**ae** 14 **eu** 45
Pontardawe	*ponn-tar-dow-ay*	**aw** 15 -**e** 43
	("dow" rhymes with "now")	
Porth Neigwl	*porth naigool*	**ei** 45 **w** 30
Rhiwlas	*roo-lass*	**iw** 51 **s** 52
Tywi	*towy*	**yw** 58
	(rhymes with "snowy")	

Now try these before you look up the rules or answers.

Bethesda	**e** 13 **s** 52
Bryn-mawr	**awr** 42
Caer-went	**aer** 41
Ffestiniog	**i** 13 **io** 49
Gorseinon	**ei** 45 **s** 52
Llan-wern	**er** 48 **ll** 25
Meifod	**ei** 45 **f** 21
Migneint	**ei** 45
Ystrad Meurig	**a** 13 **eu** 45 **y** 31

Suggested pronunciation for these is on page 64.

Answers from page 57 - *teerd, gwess-keer, dur-nodd.*

Place Name Practice – 2

These ones are a little bit harder, with more problem letters.

Aberdaron	*abbair-darronn*	**a/o** 13 **er** 48
Brynsiencyn	*brinn-shenn-kinn*	**c** 19 **si** 55 **y** 31
Cemais	*kemm-ice*	**ae** 14 **e** 13 **s** 52
Clegyr	*kleggeer*	**e** 13 **g** 24 **yr** 57
Cwmdeuddwr	*koomm-day-thooer*	**dd** 20 **eu** 45 **w** 30
Dyfed	*duvvedd*	**-ed** 44 **f** 21 **y** 31
Meirionnydd	*may-ree-onnith*	**dd** 20 **ei** 45 **io** 49
Pantrhiwgoch	*pant-roo-gauk*	**ch** 19 **iw** 51 **o** 13
Plas yn Rhiw	*plahss unn roo* ("ah" as in "ah!")	**iw** 51 **s** 52 **y** 31
Rhandir-mwyn	*rann-deer-mooinn*	**ir** 50 **w** 30 **y** 31
Scwd yr Eira	*skood a rairah* ("ah" as in "ah!")	**ei** 45 **w** 30 **y** 31,57
Tre'r Ceiri	*trair kairy*	**c** 19 **ei** 45 **er** 48
Troedrhiwdalar	*troid-roo-dallar*	**a** 13 **iw** 51 **oe** 26
Tudweiliog	*tidd-wail-yogg*	**ei** 45 **io** 49 **u** 29

Now some for you to try. Again, have a go before you look up the rule pages.

Caergwrle	**aer** 41 **-e** 43 **wr** 56
Caernarfon	**aer** 41 **f** 21 **o** 13
Caersws	**aer** 41 **s** 52 **w** 30
Ceiriog	**c** 19 **ei** 45 **io** 49
Felindre	**e** 13 **-e** 43 **f** 21
Moel Siabod	**a/o** 13 **oe** 26 **si** 55
Rhinog Fawr	**awr** 42 **f** 21 **i/o** 13
Rhosili	**i/o** 13 **s** 52
Trefriw	**e** 13 **f** 21 **iw** 51
Waunfawr	**au** 14,29 **awr** 42 **f** 21

Suggested pronunciation on page 64.

Answers from page 58 - *toe-odd, you, brith-roo*.

Place Name Practice - 3

The real heavy stuff. No room for page numbers!

Barclodiad y Gawres	*bar-klodd-yadda gow-ress* ("gow" rhymes with "now")	**a awr -es ia o y**
Beddgelert	*bathe-gellert* ("g" as in "get")	**dd e er g**
Carnedd Llywelyn	*kar-neth thloe-ellin*	**dd e ll yw**
Cyrn y Brain	*keern-a-brine*	**ai c y yr**
Glyder Fach	*gluddair vahk* ("ah" as in "ah!")	**a ch er f y**
Grwyne Fawr	*grooinn-ay vowr* (rhymes with "hour")	**awr -e f w**
Gwydyr	*gwiddeer*	**g w y yr**
Llanfairfechan	*thlann-vyre-veckann*	**a air ch e f ll**
Penrhiw-ceibr	*penn-roo-kaibair*	**c ei er iw**
Rhosllannerchrugog	*ross-thannair-kriggogg*	**ch er i ll o s u**
Trawsfynydd	*trowss-vunnith*	**aw dd f s y**
Ystradfellte	*uss-tradd-veth-tay*	**a -e f ll y**

Your turn now. No help this time - you're on your own.

Abergele
Aber-soch
Betws-y-coed
Carnedd y Filiast
Cerrigydrudion
Esgairgeiliog
Glyder Fawr
Llanfair Caereinion
Llanidloes
Llanwrtyd
Maelienydd
Tanygrisiau

Suggested pronunciation on page 65.

Place Name Practice - Answers

From page 61:

Bethesda	*beth-ess-dah*	e 13 s 52
	("ah" as in "ah!")	
Bryn-mawr	*brinn-mowr*	awr 42
	(rhymes with "hour")	
Caer-went	*kyre-went*	aer 41
Ffestiniog	*fest-inn-yogg*	i 13 io 49
Gorseinon	*gorse-ainonn*	ei 45 s 52
Llan-wern	*thlann-wairn*	er 48 ll 25
Meifod	*may-vodd*	ei 45 f 21
Migneint	*migg-naint*	ei 45
Ystrad Meurig	*uss-tradd may-rigg*	a 13 eu 45 y 31

From page 62:

Caergwrle	*kyre-gooer-lay*	aer 41 -e 43 wr 56
Caernarfon	*kyre-nar-vonn*	aer 41 f 21 o 13
Caersws	*kyre-sooss*	aer 41 s 52 w 30
Ceiriog	*kay-ree-ogg*	c 19 ei 45 io 49
Felindre	*vellinn-dray*	e 13 -e 43 f 21
Moel Siabod	*moil shabbodd*	a/o 13 oe 26 si 55
Rhinog Fawr	*rinnogg vowr*	awr 42 f 21 i/o 13
	(rhymes with "hour")	
Rhosili	*ross-illy*	i/o 13 s 52
Trefriw	*trevv-roo*	e 13 f 21 iw 51
Waunfawr	*wine-vowr*	au 14,29 awr 42 f 21
	(rhymes with "hour")	

Place Name Practice - Answers

From page 63:

Abergele	*abbair-gellay*	a/e -e er g
Aber-soch	*abbair-sawk*	a/o ch er
Betws-y-coed	*bettooss-a-koid*	e oe s w y
Carnedd y Filiast	*karneth a vill-yast*	dd e/i f ia y
Cerrigydrudion	*kerrigg-a-dridd-yonn*	c g io u y
Esgairgeiliog	*ess-kyre-gale-yogg*	air ei g io s
Glyder Fawr	*gluddair vowr*	awr er f y
	(rhymes with "hour")	
Llanfair ...	*thlann-vyre...*	air ll f
... Caereinion	*...kyre-ain-yonn*	aer ei io
Llanidloes	*thlann-idd-lois*	a ll oe s
Llanwrtyd	*thlann-ooer-tidd*	a ll wr y
Maelienydd	*mile-yennith*	ae dd e ie
Tanygrisiau	*tann-a-grish-eye*	a au i si y

End of REFINEMENTS Section

If the answers on the last two pages weren't too much of a surprise to you, that means your Welsh pronunciation is now of a very good standard. Congratulations! Have *another* cup of tea or pint of Felinfoel or something similar to celebrate - you've earned it. Then have a rest. Then have a go at the next section. A bit harder this time, but if you've got this far, you'll be OK.

If you still don't feel too sure, have the cup of tea or the pint of Felinfoel and the rest anyway, then have a quick run through the rules and the place name practice again. It'll probably click this time.

More English words in Welsh

Answers from page 59:

ambulance	balance	bamboo
bike	brake	buses
clear	case	cocktail
council	cool	curtains
the movie	date	dole
doubt	express	anyway
aeroplane	vicar	flakes
fluke	floodlight	fortune
front	game	gravy
great	group	guts
humour	interview	yacht
line-up	navy blue	nice
number	nurse	ounce
pint	pickle	puce
policy	process	punk
rice	right	rough guide
saloon	celluloid	scarcely believe
scrum	scoop	shampoo
shock	shop	sugar
sure	suit	sly
sausage	style	strike
streak	suburb	tiles
train	tunnel	tourist
tough	weekend	uncle

The Works

In this section you'll find an explanation of the trickier parts of Welsh pronunciation. The rule page format of the earlier sections isn't always the best way to present this, so from now on there will be more variety and more detail.

There is a lot in this section - in fact it gives you all you need to know about Welsh pronunciation except the very obscure points. It's up to you how much of it you decide to use and how much you decide to ignore. Every bit you use will make your pronunciation just a little better.

There's a limit, of course, to how far you can go in Welsh pronunciation just by using a book. If you want to get a really good accent, there's nothing for it but to buy a cassette, listen to native speakers or tune in to Welsh language radio and TV. You might not be able to find a cassette for place names, but for general Welsh pronunciation, you should be able to buy the cassette that goes with *Teach Yourself Welsh* at any large bookshop.

If you follow the rules given in this section, you should find that people anywhere in Wales will understand your pronunciation. You might not always find it quite so easy to understand theirs. There are a lot of different accents in Wales. This book is based on what most Southerners would think of as the "correct" pronunciation of place names. In the North you may find people using the Welsh "a" sound instead of "ae", "ai", "au" or "e" at or near the end of a word. In the South you will often hear people pronouncing "ae", "ai" or "au" at the end of a word as a Welsh "e". In the North also "u" and "y" don't sound quite like "i". This northern "u" sound is impossible to describe - you'll just have to wait till you hear it.

THE WORKS

Vowels, Syllables, Accent

Before you go any further, you need to know the meanings of these technical terms. If you already do, skip the bits with headings in square brackets.

Vowels

In Welsh the letters "a", "e", "i", "o", "u", "w" and "y" count as "vowels". All other letters count as "consonants".

(That's not the whole truth, but it'll do to be going on with.)

By the way, don't let anyone tell you there are words in Welsh with no vowels. There are some languages that have words with no vowels (the Berbers in North Africa say "ttss" for "sleep") but Welsh isn't one of them. Words like **dŵr**, "water", have the vowel "w".

[Syllables]

The notion of "syllables" has to do with the way the vowels and consonants are arranged in a word.

If you take the word "pronouncing", for example, and pick out the vowels in capitals, you get:

pr.O.n.OU.nc.I.ng

So in this word the consonants come between the vowels and split them up in such a way that there are three separate places in the word where there are vowels: .O. - .OU. - .I. Another way of putting this is to say that the word has three "syllables".

Some more examples:

m.A.n	just one vowel - one syllable.
m.AI.n	two vowels but both together in one place - still only one syllable.
m.I.n.I.ng	two vowels, separated by the consonant "n" - two syllables.
m.EA.n.I.ng	three vowels in two groups separated by the consonant "n" - two syllables.

But if there are more than two vowels together in one place, they usually count as two syllables - for example:

s.EE.I.ng	three vowels together, two syllables.

Syllables in Welsh

In Welsh three vowels together count as only one syllable if the first is "i" or "w". So **waun** is one syllable and **ciliau** is two syllables. On the other hand, two vowels together count as two syllables if they are not one of the pairs listed in the rule pages in this book. So **Coed-duon** is three syllables, because there isn't a rule page for "uo".

So how many syllables are there in these Welsh words?

blaen	dinas	mawr
mynydd	neuadd	Caeathro
Dduallt	Eglwyswrw	Mawddach
Pwllheli	Tanygrisiau	Teifi
Trearddur	Cerrigydrudion	

See bottom of page 73 for suggested answers.

Long Vowels

* How do long vowels sound?

All Welsh vowels have at least two different sounds, a "short" sound and a "long" sound. The short sound is the one to use most of the time, but the long sound pops up now and again.

"a", "e", "i", "o":

The short sounds of "a", "e", "i" and "o" are as in "pat", "pet", "pit" and "pot". These are the sounds you know already from the BASICS section. The long sound of "a" is as in "father" and the long sound of "i" is as in "machine" - like English "ee". Long "o" is like English "au" and long "e" is a bit like the first "e" in "fete" - or English "ay" - but much more like French "e" as in "pere". The word "air" as pronounced in England is pretty close to this sound, but there mustn't be any hint of an "r"!

"u":

"u", as usual, works exactly the same as "i".

"w":

"w" has long and short sounds that match the two different "oo" sounds in English You didn't know there were two different "oo" sounds in English? Well, there are. The short sound comes in words like "foot" and "good", and also in some words with a "u" like "put" and "full". The long sound comes in words like "cool" and "room", and also in some words with a "u" like "rule" and "flute".

If you say the words "pull" and "pool" out loud, you should be able to hear that they're the same except that "pull" has the short Welsh "w" sound and "pool" has the long Welsh "w" sound. But just to be difficult, if you compare "look" and "Luke", "look" has the short "w" sound and "Luke" has the long "w" sound. That's English spelling for you! (Be careful if you come from Lancashire or Cheshire, where "look" and "Luke" sound the same.)

"y":

"y" is a bit more complicated - in fact it's one of the only two real nuisances in Welsh spelling (the other is "w"). See later.

* Where do you find long vowels?

You will only find long vowels in words of one syllable. Even then the vowel will usually be short if all there is after it is one of these:

"c", "l", "m", "n", "ng", "p", "r", "t"

or if it's followed by more than one consonant.

Sometimes you'll see the sign "^" over a vowel. That means the vowel is long. The name of this sign, as you'll know if you've come across it before, is "circumflex accent", but the Welsh call it **to bach**, *toe bahk*, "little roof".

Bear in mind that "w" almost always has the *short* sound in Welsh. So for example the "wl" in **Ynys-y-bwl** rhymes with "pull", not "pool".

Answers to "How many syllables?", page 71:

blaen	1	di-nas	2	mawr	1
my-nydd	2	neu-add	2	Cae-ath-ro	3
Ddu-allt	2	Eg-lwys-w-rw	4	Maw-ddach	2
Pwll-hel-i	3	Tan-y-gri-siau	4	Tei-fi	2
Tre-ar-ddur	3	Ce-rrig-y-drud-ion	5		

Y in the Last Syllable

In earlier sections a different pronunciation was given for "y" "when it's near the end of a word". You may have thought at the time that seemed a bit too vague. It was. The proper rule is that "y" sounds different when it's in the *last syllable* of a word - and that includes words of one syllable, except the little words like **y**, **yn** etc. that were listed earlier.

	Last syllable	Anywhere else
"y"	like Welsh "i"	like "u" in "cut"
"yr"	"ear"	"ur" as in "fur"
"yw"	"you"	"oh"

(This is the closest English spelling can get to the sounds of "yr" and "yw". More about this later.)

When "y" is in the last syllable, it can be long or short just as "i" can, and for the same reasons. So in **blodyn**, "flower", pronounced *bloddinn*, it's short because the word has more than one syllable. In **bryn**, "hill", pronounced *brinn*, it's short because it's followed by "n". But in **rhyd**, "ford", pronounced (roughly) *reed*, it's long because it isn't followed by one of the letters "c" "l" "m" etc.

Examples of short vowels:

Banc	bank	*bank*
Bron	slope	*bronn*
Bryn	hill	*brinn*
Cam	crooked	*kamm*
Cil	corner	*kill*
Cist	coffer	*kist*
Crwn	round	*kroonn* (short)
Cwm	valley	*koomm* (short)
Cyll	hazel trees	*kith*
Ffin	boundary	*finn*
Gallt	hill	*gath-t*
Glan	bank, shore	*glann*
Gwyn	white, fair	*gwinn*
Gwynt	wind	*gwint*
Pen	top	*penn*
Pont	bridge	*pont*
Pum	five	*pimm*
Pwll	pit, pool	*pooth* (short)
Sant	saint	*sant*
Tal	end	*tal* (rhymes with "pal")
Twlc	pigsty	*toolk* (short)

Examples of long vowels:

Bach	small	*bahk* ("ah" as in "ah!)
Bedd	grave	*bathe* (*bairthe* in England)
Bod	dwelling	*baud*
Brith	mottled	*breeth*
Coch	red	*kauk*
Cog	cuckoo	*kaug*
Crug	hillock	*kreeg*
Du	black	*dee*
Ffridd	pasture, alp	*freethe*
Ffrwd	stream	*frood* (long)
Glas	blue	*glahss* ("ah" as in "ah!")
Gof	smith	*gauv*
Gwig	wood	*gweeg*
Is	lower	*eess*

Llech	slate	*thlake (thlairke* in England)
Llys	court	*thleess*
Rhos	moor	*rauss*
Rhyd	ford	*reed*
Sych	dry	*seek*
Teg	fair	*taig (tairg* in England)
Tre	town	*tray (trair* in England)
Tref	town	*trave (trairve* in England)
Tri	three	*tree*
Ty	house	*tee*

Now, how would you pronounce these:

Bwlch	gap, pass
Clyd	sheltered
Din	fort
Ffos	ditch
Grug	hillock,heather
Llan	church
Lle	place
Llyn	lake
Moch	pigs
Nant	brook
Plas	mansion
Pren	timber
Pridd	soil
Scwd	waterfall
Ton	waste land

See page 79 for suggested answers

[Accent/Stress]

When a word has more than one syllable, one of the syllables is usually sounded more strongly than the others.

For example, if someone is charged with a crime, the court may decide to *convict* him (or, occasionally, her). If this happens, he (or, occasionally, she) goes to gaol and becomes a *convict*.

The word *convict* is spelt the same both times, but it sounds different. The first time it appears, the "-vict" part is sounded more strongly than the "con-" part. You could show this by writing it "conVICT". The second time, the "con-" part is sounded more strongly than the "-vict" part, so you could write it "CONvict". Try saying the two versions out loud to hear the difference.

If you say that the "accent", or the "stress", is on a particular syllable, it means that syllable is sounded more strongly than the other syllables in the word.

Accent in Welsh

The rule in Welsh is that the accent is normally on the *second to last syllable* of a word.

So, for example, **Ystradgynlais** (Y.str.A.d - g.Y.n - l.AI.s) has four groups of vowels, Y-A-Y-AI, and the second to last of these groups is the second Y, so it's pronounced "ystradGYNlais" with the stress on the second to last syllable, "GYN".

Compound words

Most Welsh placenames are compound words - that is, they're made up of several shorter words strung together. For example, **Pont-rhyd-y-groes** is "bridge-of-ford-of-the-crossroads", and **Llantysilio** is llan-Tysilio, "church-of-Tysilio".

(The list of Place Name Elements at the end of the book will usually show you how to split up a name into individual words.)

This affects the pronunciation of "y" and it also affects the accent. **Pont-rhyd-y-groes** is four syllables (p.O.nt - rh.Y.d - .Y. - gr.OE.s) and the last syllable is GROES, so the two "y'"s are not in the last syllable and you'd expect them to be pronounced as "u" in "cut". But the first "y" is in the word **rhyd** ("ford"), and *in that word* it *is* in the last syllable, so that syllable is pronounced (roughly) *reed* (*long* "y" because the last letter is not "c" "l" "m" etc.). The second "y" is the word **y**, "the", which is one of those little words mentioned earlier that have the "u" as in "cut" pronunciation, so this time you *should* pronounce it as *uh*.

Likewise, you'd expect the accent to be on the second to last syllable, the second "y". But because this is the word **y**, "the", which is an unimportant little word that people skip over quickly, you can't put the accent there. The only other place you can put the accent in a Welsh word is the last syllable, so **Pont-rhyd-y-groes** has to be accented "pont-rhyd-y-GROES". The pronunciation of the whole word would be, roughly, *pont-reed-a-GROISS*.

In **Llantysilio**, on the other hand, the second to last syllable is SIL, which is also the second to last syllable of the name **Tysilio**, so it has the accent. Likewise the "y" isn't in the last syllable of **Tysilio**, so it can be pronounced as "u" in "cut". So the whole word is pronounced (roughly) *thlann-tuss-ILL-yo*.

So where is the accent in these names?

Afon-wen	**Basaleg**	**Danygraig**
Maentwrog	**Pentrefelin**	**Pontardawe**

See bottom of page 80 for suggested answers.

Suggested pronunciation for long and short vowels, from page 76:

Bwlch	gap, pass	*boolk* (short)
Clyd	sheltered	*kleed*
Din	fort	*dinn*
Ffos	ditch	*fauss*
Grug	hillock, heather	*greeg*
Llan	church	*thlann*
Lle	place	*thlay* (*thlair* in England)
Llyn	lake	*thlinn*
Moch	pigs	*mauk*
Nant	brook	*nant*
Plas	mansion	*plahss* ("ah" as in "ah!")
Pren	timber	*prenn*
Pridd	soil	*preethe*
Scwd	waterfall	*skood* (long)
Ton	waste land	*tonn*

"Correct" pronunciation

As you gathered earlier, there are some difficult sounds in Welsh which you don't have to get 100% right. In previous sections you were shown how to get round these by using the nearest familiar English sound. In this section you'll get the chance to aim for the fully correct pronunciation of these sounds. You may find there are some that you can't manage. No problem. Just stick with what you learnt in the earlier sections.

In this section there very often won't be any suggested answers because most of these sounds can't be shown in English spelling. For the same reason, when the sound of a Welsh word is shown in English spelling, the "incorrect" version of these sounds will still be given, but in **heavy type** to remind you that it's not quite right.

The one sound not mentioned in this section is "ll". If you found it hard the first time round and want to have another go at it, see "A Challenge", page 8.

Answers to accent question on page 78:

Afon-WEN	**Ba-SAL-eg**	**Dany-GRAIG**
Maen-TWR-og	**Pentre-FEL-in**	**Pontar-DAW-e**

ch

For many English speakers this is the hardest Welsh sound of all. Nobody's going to blame you if you give up on it - but why not at least have a go?

It's the same as:

> Scottish "ch" in words like "loch"
> German "ch" in words like "achtung"
> Spanish "j" or "x" in words like "hijo" or "Mexico"
> Irish "gh" in names like "Haughey"

It's a bit like an English "h", but rougher - as you blow gently for the "h", you have to do a bit of a gargle in your throat. If you're doing it properly you should feel the back of your throat grating.

It helps a lot of you can listen to someone who already knows how to do it - a Welsh speaker, a Scot, a German, a Spaniard, an Irish person etc.

You can practise it using any of the words you've already had that contain this sound:

chwil	**chwip**	**cylch**
Aber-soch	**Amlwch**	**Bylchau**
Crymych	**Glyder Fach**	**Llanfairfechan**
Llechwedd	**Machynlleth**	**Maenclochog**
Mawddach	**Pantrhiwgoch**	and (wait for it ...)

Rhosllannerchrugog!

dd

"Th" in English has two different sounds. English speakers spell these two sounds the same, but Welsh speakers spell them differently - one is "th", the other is "dd". To get "dd" right, you need to be able to tell the difference.

When someone puts a sword in its "sheath" (not a common event, admittedly), we say that they "sheathe" it. The two words "sheath" and "sheathe" sound exactly the same except for the two different "th" sounds. If you say the two words to yourself, you should easily be able to tell which is which. But if you leave off the "-th" and "-the", you'll find the two words sound the same - they both sound like "she".

The "th" in "sheath" is the Welsh "th", the "th" in "sheathe" is the Welsh "dd".

Another example - "thistle" and "this'll" (as in "This'll do"). Again, the only difference in sound is the two versions of "th". If you can hear the difference, try leaving off the "th-" (saying "-istle" and "-is'll") and see if you can still hear a difference. The "th" in "thistle" is the Welsh "th", the "th" in "this'll" is the Welsh "dd".

In general you find the Welsh "dd" sound at the beginning of very common little English words like "the", "this", "that", "then", "they" etc. (but not "thin"), and also between vowels in words like "father", "mother", "weather" (but be careful - in "nothing" the sound is the Welsh "th"). English words ending in "-the" also usually have the "dd" sound - compare "breath" with "breathe", "bath" with "bathe" etc.

Bear in mind that this applies to "dd" *anywhere* in a Welsh word, not just at the beginning.

Examples:

bedd	grave	*bathe* (*bairthe* in England)
ddau	two	*thy*
ddu	black	*thee*
blaidd	wolf	*blythe*
brudd	sad	*breathe*

Now, how would you pronounce these?

haidd	barley
sudd	juice
ddaw	come

See bottom of page 86 for suggested answers.

(A clue - as with the examples above, for each of these three words there is an English word that sounds almost exactly like it.)

ei, eu

This isn't a very important page - skip it if you're in a hurry.

Strictly speaking, these should sound like a very quick "uh" sound followed by a "y". It's the same sound as in French words like "oeil" or "feuille". People from the West Country sometimes use this sound in words like "eye", "like", "fight" and so on, so if you can put on a sort of tacky "zyder vrom Zummerzet" accent and say these words, you'll get a good idea of the Welsh pronunciation. (And it might help you with "r" as well.)

But don't despair if you can't do it. You'll hear Welsh people pronounce "ei" and "eu" in all sorts of ways - "ee", "ay", "eye" etc. So "ay" will do nicely.

If you find you can do it, practise it in some of the words you've had already:

beudy	**deu**	**eithin**
heulog	**ieir** (help!)	**meibion**
Ceiriog	**Cwmdeuddwr**	**Gorseinon**
Llandeilo	**Migneint**	**Nant yr Eira**
Tudweiliog	**Ystradmeurig**	and (wait for it...)

Penrhyndeudraeth!

ew, iw/uw/yw, ow

(To recap, "uw" sounds exactly like "iw", and "yw" sounds exactly like "iw" when it's in the last syllable of a word)

To understand how these sound, imagine a small child who has a "weak r" and says "wabbit" instead of "rabbit".

If this child tried to say "terrible", it would end up with something that you might spell as "tewwible". This is exactly the sound of the Welsh "ew".

This isn't too bad for an English person when the next letter is a vowel, as in the name **Dewi** (David). This is as if our small child tried to say "Derry" and ended up with "Dewwy". Likewise **newydd** (new) is pronounced (roughly) *newwith*, as if the small child was trying to say "nerrith".

The difficulty comes when you try to put the same sound in words like **cewri** (giants) or **tew** (fat) where there isn't a vowel after the "ew". Try saying "tewwible" and then leaving out the "-ible" bit.

Likewise for "iw", imagine the same child trying to say "irritating". It would come out as "iwwitating". This is the sound in Welsh words like **rhiw**.

The same goes for "ow". Imagine the child saying "horrible". It would come out as "howwible". So the county name **Powys** sounds like the child trying to say "porriss" and coming out with "powwiss".

You can practise these sounds in some of the words you've had already, and a few new ones:

Huw	rhiw	tiwb
distryw	Dowlais	Efailnewydd
Llandowror	Rhiwlas	Sirhowy
Trefriw	Ystradowen	and (wait for it ...)

Troedrhiwdalar!

Suggested pronunciation of "dd", from page 83:)

haidd	barley	*hythe*
sudd	juice	*seethe*
ddaw	come	*thou*

r

In English as spoken in England (apart from the West Country and parts of Lancashire) the letter "r" is sounded quite weakly or, very often, not at all. For example, "farther" sounds just the same as "father" and "shorn" sounds just the same as "Shaun".

In Welsh "r" is always sounded strongly and is usually trilled. Many Scots sound their "r"'s like this - they say things like "R-r-r-really?" English people often find they can't do it. If you're doing it properly, you'll feel the tip of your tongue vibrating against the roof of your mouth. A lot of Irish people can do it, and Americans and people from the English West Country can get quite close to it.

Even if you can't trill your "r"'s, you can improve your Welsh pronunciation with the following trick:

In English as spoken in England the letter "r" tends to get completely lost when there isn't a vowel immediately after it. You can hear the "r" in "earache" but not in "ear" or "earmuff". (Try it.)

When you find a Welsh word where there's an "r" without a vowel straight after it, try doubling the "r" and adding an "a".

For example, **Gorseinon**. Most English people would tend to pronounce this *gaw-sainonn*. Double the "r" – "GoRR-seinon" - and add an "a" – "GoRRA-seinon". Now say *gorra-sainonn* very quickly so that you can hardly hear the "a" at all.

Try the same thing with **Bangor** - *bang-gorra*. The "a" has to be so short that it almost isn't there. If you can get the same "r" sound without the "a" being heard at all, so much the better.

If there are two vowels immediately before the "r", you don't need to double it. Just add the "a". So for **Caerwent,** you make it "CaerAwent" and pronounce it *kyra-went*, skipping over the "a" as quickly as possible.

More examples (the extra "a" is in brackets):

Abergele	*abberr(a)g-ellay*
Caergwrle	*kyr(a)-goorr(a)-lay* (short "oo")
Caernarfon	*kyr(a)-narr(a)-vonn*
Cwmdeuddwr	*koomm-day-thoor(a)* (short "oo")
Cyrn y Brain	*kirr(a)n-a-brine*
Glyder Fawr	*gludderr(a) vow-r(a)*
Gwydir	*gwidd-irr(a)*
Llanbadarn	*thlann-baddarr(a)n*
Llanwern	*thlann-werr(a)n*
Merthyr	*merr(a)-thirr(a)*
Porth Neigwl	*porr(a)th naigooll* (short "oo")
Rhandir-mwyn	*rann-dirr(a)-mooinn*
Tre'r Ceiri	*trerr(a) kairy*
Waunfawr	*wine-vow-r(a)*

Now, how would you pronounce these?

Aberdaron
Beddgelert
Bryn-mawr
Carnedd Dafydd
Claerwen
Clegyr
Gorseinon
Hirwaun
Llanfairfechan
Llanwrtyd
Ogwr
Penrhiw-ceibr
Pontardawe
Porthmadog

See bottom of page 90 for suggested answers.

rh

This isn't a very important page - skip it if you're in a hurry.

Strictly speaking, "rh" is exactly what it says - a Welsh "r" followed by an "h". In other words, after the "r", you just blow gently. In practice many Welsh-speaking people blow just before the "r" rather than just after it, so it sounds as "hr", not "rh".

If you find this hard to do, you'll be pleased to hear that a lot of Welsh-speaking people leave the "h" out altogether, so there's no reason why you shouldn't do the same.

You can practise on the following names that you've already had:

Henrhyd	**Llanrhidian**	**Pistyll Rhaeadr**
Plas yn Rhiw	**Rhandir-mwyn**	**Rheidol**
Rhinog Fawr	**Rhuddlan**	and (of course ...)

Rhosllannerchrugog! (sounds familiar?)

Suggested pronunciation of words with "r", from page 88:

Aberdaron	*abberr(a)-darronn*
Beddgelert	*bathe-gellerr(a)t*
	("g" as in "get")
Bryn-mawr	*brinn mow-r(a)*
	("mow" rhymes with "now")
Carnedd Dafydd	*karr(a)-neth davvith*
Claerwen	*klyr(a)-wenn*
Clegyr	*kleggirr(a)*
Gorseinon	*gorr(a)-sainonn*
Hirwaun	*hirr(a)-wine*
Llanfairfechan	*thlann-vyr(a)-veckann*
Llanwrtyd	*thlann-oorr(a)-tidd* (short "oo")
Ogwr	*ogg-oorr(a)* (short "oo")
Penrhiw-ceibr	*penn-roo-kaiberr(a)*
Pontardawe	*ponn-tarr(a)-dow-ay* ("dow" rhymes with "now")
Porthmadog	*porr(a)th-maddogg*

a, e, i, o
(unstressed)

In English as spoken in England, and sometimes elsewhere too, when these vowels are in an unstressed syllable (a syllable without accent, or stress) you hardly hear them at all. If you say the words:

Roman   garden   basin   bacon

you'll see that the "-an", "-en", "-in" and "-on" all sound more or less like "-un", or even "'n'" as in "fish 'n' chips".

(This happens much more often with "a", "e" and "o" than with "i".)

This doesn't happen in Welsh. These letters have the same sound in any syllable, stressed or unstressed. So, for example, **Rheidol** is not pronounced "raidle", as it might be in English, but more or less as the two English words "ray-doll". Likewise the name **Megan** is pronounced like the two English names "Meg-Ann". **Dinas**, "city", is pronounced *din-ass* and **ffynnon**, "well", is pronounced *fun-on*.

More examples:

awel	*ow-ell*	**Breidden**	*bray-then*
caban	*cab-ann*	**Cadfan**	*cad-van*
Clocaenog	*clock-eye-nog*	**coelbren**	*coil-bren*
Dyfed	*dove-ed*	**Elan**	*ell-ann*
Ffrancon	*frank-on*	**hafod**	*have-odd*
heulog	*hay-log*	**Pennant**	*pen-ant*
Rhiwlas	*rue-lass*	**Tanat**	*tan-at*

Now try these yourself:

afon	Aman	caled	canol
carnedd	carreg	cawres	collen
Madog	Mathrafal	Mihangel	neuadd
pentref	trindod	uchaf	ystrad

-a, -e, -o, -w

When the letters "a", "e" and "o" come at the end of a word of more than one syllable, they still have the short pronunciation.

For example, in **Rhondda**, the "a" on the end is pronounced roughly as in "pat". It's as if the word was pronounced *ron-that* and then the "t" at the end was left off without changing the sound of the "a" - *ron-tha'*.

Likewise, **Hepste** is pronounced roughly like *hep-step* with the final "p" left off - *hep-ste'*.

And **Carno** is pronounced roughly like *car-not* with the "t" left off - *car-no'*.

The same thing happens with "w", but this is even harder for an English speaker to get used to.

The word **ceirw**, "deer", is pronounced roughly as *kay-rook* with the "k" left off - *kay-roo'*.

You can practise these sounds in these words:

garw	**bedw**	**cartre**	**morfa**
Tawe	**Teilo**	**derw**	**isa**
Mellte	**hendra**	**Tudno**	**Tysilio**

-l, -n, -r

Sometimes in Welsh the letters "l", "n" and "r" come at the end of a word without a vowel right in front of them. For example:

congl corner
cefn   ridge
Pedr   Peter

The trick here is to work backwards from the "l", "n" or "r" until you find a vowel, then copy that vowel to just before the "l", "n" or "r".

For example:

Congl - working backwards from the "l", the first (and indeed only) vowel you find is "o" (c**O**ngl), so copy that to just before the "l" (c**O**ng**O**l) and pronounce it as if it was **congol** (*kong-oll*).

So **Rhosneigr** is pronounced as if it was **Rhosneigir** - *ross-naigeer*.

A similar case is **Dyfrdwy**, pronounced as if it was **Dyfyrdwy** - *duvver-dooey*.

Now try these:

budr   **llethr**   **rhaeadr**
Cefncoed **Eifl**   **Llangynidr**

See bottom of page 98 for suggested answers.

ng

Example: **cangen**   branch   *kang-enn*

Rule: Pronounce "ng", not "ng-g".

* "Finger" is pronounced "fing-ger" - you can hear the "g". "Singer" (in most areas) is pronounced "sing-er" – you can't hear the "g". Welsh "ng" is as in "singer".
* But **Bangor** is pronounced (roughly) *bang-gor*.
* And this rule doesn't apply when the "n" and the "g" are in different words. For example, in **Llangollen**, which is really **Llan-gollen** ("church-of-hazel-tree"), the "g" is sounded.

More examples:

dringon	climbed	*dring-onn*
onglog	angular	*ong-logg*

Now, how would you pronounce these?

angen	need
Ingli	(person's name)

See bottom of page 98 for suggested answers.

W

This isn't a very important page - skip it if you're in a hurry.

At the beginning of THE WORKS the Welsh vowels were listed as "a" "e" "i" "o" "u" "w" "y" with the note "That's not the whole truth".

The whole truth is that two of the vowels, "i" and "w", can also sometimes be consonants.

"i" is a consonant in words like **Iestyn**, where it sounds like an English "y" (*yess-tinn*), and "w" is a consonant in words like **gwyn** where it sounds like an English "w" (*gwinn*).

That's why the word **gwaun** is only one syllable. It has only two vowels in it, not three, because the "w" is a consonant.

In a few words that begin with "gwl-", "gwn-" or "gwr-", the "w" is pronounced like an English "w", not like an English "oo". The "w" in these words is sounded very quickly, so that you hardly hear it, and thus "gwl-" sounds almost like "gl-", "gwn-" sounds almost like "gn"-" (you have to sound both the "g" and the "n") and "gwr-" sounds almost like "gr-".

An example everyone knows is the name **Gwladys**, which most English people spell and pronounce Gladys (*gladdiss*). To get more or less the right Welsh sound, you have to say *g(oo)laddiss*, but make the "oo" *very* short.

wy

"w" and "y" are the two big nuisances in Welsh spelling, and they're never worse than when they get together.

The simple rule is - when in doubt, say "ooey".

The main exceptions are:

1) "gwy-" is pronounced as if it was "gwi-". So **gwyn**, "white", is pronounced as if it was **gwin**. And **wyn**, which is the same word, is pronounced as if it was **win** in words like **Colwyn** and **Berwyn**.

2) If there is a vowel before the "w", the "w" goes with that vowel according to the other rules in this book and the "y" is pronounced as usual. So **tywyll**, "dark", follows the rule for "yw" - *toe-ith*.

There are a few other exceptions which you're unlikely to come across in place names.

More examples:

Conwy	(river)	*konn-ooey*
Gwydir	(village)	*gwiddeer*
Powys	(county)	*pow-iss*

Now, how would you pronounce these?

ystwyth	winding
gwynt	wind
newydd	new

See bottom of page 118 for suggested answers.

End of THE WORKS Section

Got all that? At least you now know the worst that Welsh pronunciation can throw at you. A fitting way, perhaps, to end this section. And the main part of the book. Congratulations on sticking it out. Hopefully you enjoyed it - you certainly deserved to.

If you want some place name practice, try choosing a page in the Alphabetical List of Place Names, putting a sheet of paper over the right-hand column and pronouncing the names in the left-hand column. There shouldn't be any by now that you can't do.

The next step? Learn Welsh, of course! Try *Colloquial Welsh* by Gareth King.

******

Answers from page 94 - *biddeer, thlethair, rye-addar, kevvenn-koid, aivill, thlann-gunny-deer.*

Answers from page 95 - *ang-enn, ing-lee.*

Full List of Rules

99

Instant Welsh Place Names

Alphabetical List of Welsh Place Names

Names marked * are those where the spelling (and sometimes the pronunciation) has already been changed in the past to make it more "English". Names of this sort don't follow any fixed rules. There are more of these than you'll find in this list. Any name which has a "k" or a "v" in it, or ends with "-ey", is likely to be one of these, and should be pronounced in an English way.

Abbeycwmhir	*abbey-koomm-heer*
Aberaeron	*abbair-eye-ronn*
Abercynon	*abbair-kunnonn*
*Aberdare	*abber-dare*
Aberdaron	*abbair-darronn*
*Aberdovey	*abber-duvvy*
Aberedw	*abb-erredd-oo*
Abereiddi	*abb-erray-thee*
Aber-erch	*abbair-airk*
Aber-fan	*abbair-vann*
Aberffraw	*abbair-frow* (rhymes with "now")
Aber-ffrwd	*abbair-frood* (rhymes with "brood")
*Abergavenny	*abber-gavenny*
Abergele	*abbair-gellay* ("g" as in "get")
Aberglaslyn	*abbair-glass-linn*
Abergwesyn	*abbair-gwessinn*
Abergwili	*abbair-gwilly*
Abergwyngregyn	*abbair-gwinn-gregginn*
Abergynolwyn	*abbair-gunn-ollwinn*
Aberhafesb	*abbair-havvesp*
Aberhosan	*abbair-hossann*
Aber-soch	*abbair-sawk*
Abersychan	*abbair-suckann*
*Abertillery	*abber-till-airy*
Abertridwr	*abbair-tridd-ooer*
Aberystwyth	*abb-erruss-tooith*
Aeron	*eye-ronn*

Afon-wen	*avvonn-wenn*
Aman	*ammann*
Amlwch	*amm-look*
Amroth	*amm-roth*
Aran	*arrann*
Arenig Fach	*arrennigg vahk* ("ah" as in "ah!")
Arenig Fawr	*arrennigg vowr* (rhymes with "hour")
Argoed	*argoid*
Arthog	*arthog*
Arwystli	*arrooist-lee*
Bagillt	*baggith-t*
Baglan	*bagg-lann*
Bala	*ballah* ("ball" as in "ballot", "ah" as in "ah!")
Bancffosfelen	*bank-foss-vellenn*
Bancycapel	*bank-a-kappell*
Bancyfelin	*bank-a-vellinn*
Bangor	*bang-gor*
Bangor Is-coed	*bang-gor-eess-koid*
Bangor Is-y-coed	*bang-gor-eess-a-koid*
Bangor Teifi	*bang-gor-tavy*
Barclodiad y Gawres	*bar-klodd-yadda gow-ress* ("gow" rhymes with "now")
Bargoed	*bargoid*
*Barry	*barry*
Basaleg	*bass-allegg* ("all" as in "alley")
Beddgelert	*bathe-gellairt* ("g" as in "get")
Bedlinog	*bedd-linnogg*
Bedwas	*bedd-wass* (rhymes with "lass")
Bedwellte	*bedd-wethte*
Benllech	*benn-thleck*
Berwyn	*bair-winn*
Bethesda	*beth-ess-dah* ("ah" as in "ah!")
Betws Garmon	*bettooss garmonn*
Betws Gwerful Goch	*bettooss gwair-vill gauk*
Betws-y-coed	*bettooss-a-koid*
Blaenau Ffestiniog	*bline-eye fest-inn-yogg*
*Blaenavon	*bline-avvunn*
Blaen-plwyf	*bline-plooivv*
Blaina	*bline-ah* ("ah" as in "ah!")

*Blorenge	*blorrenj*
Bodelwyddan	*boddell-ooey-than*
Bodfari	*bodd-varry*
Bodnant	*bodd-nant*
Boduan	*bodd-eeann*
Boncath	*bonn-kath*
Bontdolgadfan	*bont doll-gadd-vann*
Bont Rhydgaled	*bont reed-galledd* ("gall" as in "galley")
Borth-y-gest	*borth-a-guest*
Botwnnog	*bott-oonnogg*
Braich y Pwll	*brike a pooth*
Brechfa	*breck-vah* ("ah" as in "ah!")
*Brecon	*breckunn*
Breiddin	*bray-thin*
Brithdir	*brith-deer* ("brith" rhymes with "pith")
Broniarth	*bronn-yarth*
Bronllys	*bronn-thleess*
Brymbo	*brumm-bo*
Brynaber	*brinn-abbair*
Brynaman	*brinn-ammann*
Bryn Amlwg	*brinn-amm-loogg*
Bryn-celli-ddu	*brinn kethly thee*
Bryncir	*brinn-keer*
Bryn-coch	*brinn-cauk*
Bryneglwys	*brinn-egg-lewis*
Bryn-mawr	*brinn-mowr* (rhymes with "hour")
Brynsiencyn	*brinn-shenn-kinn*
Bryn-teg	*brinn-taig*
*Builth	*billth*
Bwlchtocyn	*boolk-tockinn*
Bwlch-y-Sarnau	*boolk-a-sarn-eye*
Bylchau	*bulk-eye*
Caban-coch	*kabbann-kawk*
Cadair Idris	*kaddire idd-riss* ("ire" rhymes with "fire")
Caeathro	*kye-athro*
Caehopcyn	*kye-hopkin*
Caergwrle	*kyre-gooer-lay*
*Caerleon	*kare-leeunn*
Caernarfon	*kyre-nar-vonn*
*Caerphilly	*kare-filly*

Caersws	*kyre-sooss*
Caer-went	*kyre-went*
Caerwys	*kyre-ooiss*
Capel Curig	*kappell kirrigg*
Capel Garmon	*kappell garmonn*
Capel-y-ffin	*kappell-a-finn*
*Carmarthen	*kar-marthen*
Carnedd Dafydd	*karneth davvith*
Carnedd Llywelyn	*karneth thloe-ellinn*
Carnedd y Filiast	*karneth a vill-yast*
Carn Ingli	*karn ing-lee*
Carn-Llidi	*karn-thliddy*
Carno	*karno*
Carreg Cennen	*karregg kennenn*
Carreg Wastad	*karregg-wass-tadd* ("wass" rhymes with "pass")
Carreg yr Imbill	*karregg a rimm-bith*
Castell Coch	*kass-teth cauk*
Castell Collen	*kass-teth koth-lenn*
Castell Dinas Brân	*kass-teth dinnass brann*
Castell y Bere	*kass-teth a berray*
Cefn-coed	*kevvenn-koid*
Cefn Sidan	*kevvenn siddann*
Cegidfa	*kegg-idd-vah* ("ah" as in "ah!")
Ceiriog	*kay-ree-ogg*
Cenarth	*kenn-arth*
Cemais	*kemm-ice*
Ceredigion	*kerredd-igg-yonn*
Cerrigydrudion	*kerrigg-a-dridd-yonn*
Chwilog	*kwillogg*
Cilcennin	*kill-kenninn*
Cilgerran	*kilg-errann*
Ciliau Aeron	*killy-eye eye-ronn*
Cilmeri	*kill-merry*
Cilmery	*kill-merry*
Cil-y-cwm	*kill-a-koomm*
Claerwen	*klyre-wenn*
Cleddau	*kleth-eye*
Clegyr	*kleggeer*

Clocaenog	*klock-eye-nogg*
Clunderwen	*klinn-dare-wenn*
Clwyd	*klooidd*
Clydach	*kluddack*
Clynnog	*klunnogg*
*Clyro	*clye-ro*
Clywedog	*kloe-eddogg*
Cnicht	*k-nickt*
Coed-duon	*koy-deeonn*
Coed-poeth	*koid-poith*
Coed y Brenin	*koid a brenninn*
Coelbren	*koil-brenn*
Coety	*koety*
Colwyn	*koll-winn*
Comins Coch	*kommince kauk*
Commins Coch	*kommince kauk*
Conwy	*konn-ooey*
Corn Du	*korn dee*
Corris Uchaf	*korriss ickavv*
Corwen	*korwenn*
Cothi	*kothy*
Craig-y-nos	*krye-ga-nauss*
Craig yr Aderyn	*krye-ga radd-errinn*
Cricieth	*krick-yeth*
*Crickhowell	*krick-how-ull*
Croesor	*kroi-sore*
Crymych	*krummick*
Cwm-ann	*koomm-ann*
Cwmbrân	*koomm-brahn* ("ah" as in "ah!")
Cwmdeuddwr	*koomm-day-thooer*
Cwmfelin-fach	*koomm-vellinn-vahk*
Cwm Idwal	*koomm idd-wal* ("wal" rhymes with "pal")
Cwm Pennant	*koomm pennant*
Cwmtudu	*koomm-tiddy*
Cwm-twrch Isaf	*koomm-tooerk-issav*
Cwm-twrch Uchaf	*koomm-tooerk-ickav*
Cwmystwyth	*koomm-uss-tooith*
Cyfarthfa	*kuvv-arth-vah* ("ah" as in "ah!")
Cyfeiliog	*kuvv-ale-yogg*

Cymer	*kummair*
Cymmer	*kummair*
Cymru	*kummry*
Cyncoed	*kinn-koid*
Cynon	*kunnonn*
Cyrn y Brain	*keern-a-brine*
Danygraig	*dann-a-grye-g*
Dan yr Ogof	*dann-a-rogg-ovv*
Daugleddau	*die-gleth-eye*
Dduallt	*thee-atht*
Deganwy	*degg-ann-ooey*
Deheubarth	*day-hay-barth*
*Denbigh	*dennby*
Dinas Brân	*dinnass brann*
Dinas Emrys	*dinnass emm-riss*
Dinas Mawddwy	*dinnass mouthe-ooey*
Dinefwr	*dinn-evv-ooer*
Dinevor	*dinn-evver*
Dinorwic	*dinn-or-wick*
Dinorwig	*dinn-or-wigg*
Diserth	*dissairth*
Dolau Cothi	*doll-eye-kothy*
Dolbadarn	*doll-baddarn*
Dolbenmaen	*doll-benn-mine*
Dolforwyn	*doll-vor-winn*
Dolgarrog	*doll-garrogg*
Dolgellau	*dolg-ethl-eye*
Dôl-goch	*dole-gauk*
Dolwyddelan	*doll-ooey-thellann*
*Dovey	*duvvy*
Dowlais	*dow-lice* ("dow" rhymes with "now")
Dryslwyn	*druss-looinn*
Dulais	*dill-ice*
Dulas	*dill-ass*
Dwyfor	*dooey-vor*
Dwyryd	*dooey-reed*
Dyfed	*duvvedd*
Dyffryn Ardudwy	*duffrinn ar-diddooey*
Dyfi	*duvvy*
Dyfnant	*duvv-nant*

Dylife	*dull-ivvay*
Dyserth	*dussairth*
Dysynni	*duss-unny*
***Ebbw**	*ebboo*
Edeyrnion	*edd-airn-yonn*
Efailnewydd	*evvile-naywith* ("vile" rhymes with "smile")
Eglwyseg	*egg-lewis-egg*
Eglwyswrw	*egg-lewis-oorroo*
Elan	*ellann*
Elidir Fawr	*ell-iddeer vowr* (rhymes with "hour")
Eliseg	*ell-issegg*
Eppynt	*eppint*
Erddig	*air-thigg*
Esgairgeiliog	*ess-kyre-gale-yogg*
Faerdre	*vyre-dray*
Felindre	*vellinn-dray*
Felinfach	*vellinn-vahk* ("ah" as in "ah!")
Felinheli	*vellinn-helly*
Felinfoel	*vellinn-voil*
Ffaldybrenin	*fal-da-brenninn* ("fal" rhymes with "pal")
Ffestiniog	*fest-inn-yogg*
Foel Fras	*voil-vrahss* ("ah" as in "ah!")
Froncysyllte	*vronn-kuss-uth-tay*
Fron-goch	*vronn-gauk*
Fforest Fawr	*forrest vowr* (rhymes with "hour")
Ffostrasol	*foss-trassoll*
Ffynnongroyw	*funnonn-groyoo*
Gabalfa	*gabb-alvah* ("al" rhymes with "pal", "ah" as in "ah!")
Gamallt	*gammath-t*
Garnant	*garnant*
Garndolbenmaen	*garn-doll-benn-mine*
Gaufron	*guy-vronn*
Gelli-gaer	*gethly-gyre* ("g" as in "get" - both times)
Gellilydan	*gethly-luddann* ("g" as in "get")
Gilfach yr Halen	*gill-vahk er hallenn* ("gill" as of fish, "ah" as in "ah!", "hall" as in "hallow")
Gilwern	*gill-wairn* ("gill" as of fish)
Glanaman	*glann-ammann*

Glanhafren	*glann-havv-renn*
Gloddfa Ganol	*gloth-vah gannoll* ("ah" as in "ah!")
Glyder Fach	*gluddair vahk* ("ah" as in "ah!")
Glyder Fawr	*gluddair vowr* (rhymes with "hour")
Glyn Ceiriog	*glinn-kay-ree-ogg*
Glyndyfrdwy	*glinn-duvver-dooey*
Gorseinon	*gorse-ainonn*
Gregynog	*gregg-unnogg*
Groeslon	*groiss-lonn*
Grwyne Fach	*grooinn-ay vahk* ("ah" as in "ah!")
Grwyne Fawr	*grooinn-ay vowr* (rhymes with "hour")
Gurnos	*geer-nauss*
Gwalchmai	*gwalc-mye* ("alc" rhymes with "talc")
Gwendraeth	*gwenn-drye-th*
Gwent	*gwent*
Gwernyfed	*gwairn-uvvedd*
Gwydyr	*gwiddeer*
Gwynedd	*gwinneth*
Gwynfryn	*gwinn-vrinn*
Gwyrfai	*gweer-vye*
Gymru	*gumm-ry*
Gurnos	*gur-nauss*
Hafesb	*havv-esp*
Harlech	*harleck*
Hengoed	*henn-goid*
Henryd	*henn-reed*
Hepste	*hepp-stay*
Hirael	*hear-isle*
Hirnant	*hear-nant*
Hirwaun	*hear-wine*
Honddu	*honn-thee*
Hyddgen	*huth-genn*
Irfon	*ear-vonn*
Islwyn	*iss-looinn*
Ithon	*ith-onn*
*Lampeter	*lammpy-ter*
*Laugharne	*lock-arn*
Llanaber	*thlann-abbair*
Llanaelhaearn	*thlann-isle-high-arn*
Llanarmon	*thlann-armon*

Llanbabo	*thlann-babbo*
Llanbadarn	*thlann-baddarn*
Llanbedr	*thlann-beddair*
Llanbedrog	*thlann-bedd-rogg*
Llanberis	*thlann-berriss*
Llanbister	*thlann-biss-tair*
Llanboidy	*thlann-boidy*
Llanbryn-mair	*thlann-brinn-mire*
Llancaiach Fawr	*thlann-kye-ack vowr* (rhymes with "hour")
Llandaf	*thlann-daff*
Llandeilo	*thlann-dailo*
Llanddewibrefi	*thlann-they-we-brevvy*
Llanddeiniol	*thlann-thain-yoll*
Llanddeiniolen	*thlann-thain-yollenn*
Llandderfel	*thlann-their-vell*
Llanddona	*thlann-thonnah* ("ah" as in "ah!")
Llandinam	*thlann-dinnamm*
Llandogo	*thlann-doggo*
*Llandovery	*lann-duvvery*
Llanddowror	*thlann-doe-ror*
Llandrillo	*thlann-drithlo*
Llandrindod	*thlann-drinn-dodd*
Llandudno	*thlann-did-know*
Llandybïe	*thlann-dubb-ee-ay*
Llandysilio	*thlann-duss-ill-yo*
Llandysul	*thlann-dussill*
Llanelli	*thlann-ethly*
Llanelltud	*thlann-eth-tidd*
Llanelwedd	*thlann-ell-weth*
Llanerfyl	*thlann-air-vill*
Llanfachreth	*thlann-vack-reth*
Llanfair Caereinion	*thlann-vyre kyre-ain-yonn*
Llanfairfechan	*thlann-vyre-veckann*
Llanfair Pwllgwyngyll	*thlann-vyre pooth-gwinn-gith*
Llanfihangel-ar-arth	*thlannvy-hang-ell ar arth*
Llanfrothen	*thlann-vrothenn*
Llanfyllin	*thlann-vuth-linn*
Llangadfan	*thlann-gadd-vann*

Llangadog	*thlann-gaddogg*
Llangadwaladr	*thlann-gadd-walladar* ("wall" rhymes with "pal")
Llangamarch	*thlann-gamark*
Llangefni	*thlann-gevv-ny* ("g" as in "get")
Llangennith	*thlann-gennith* ("g" as in "get")
Llangernyw	*thlann-gairn-you*
Llangollen	*thlann-goth-lenn*
Llangrannog	*thlann-grannogg*
Llangurig	*thlann-girrigg* ("g" as in "give")
Llangybi	*thlann-gubby*
Llangynidr	*thlann-gunny-deer*
*Llanharry	*lann-harry*
Llanidloes	*thlann-idd-loiss*
Llanilar	*thlann-illar*
Llanllyfni	*thlann-thluvv-ny*
Llanmadog	*thlann-maddog*
Llan-non	*thlann-nonn*
Llanpumsaint	*thlann-pimm-sign-t*
Llanrhaeadr-ym- -Mochnant	*thlann-rye-add-rumm- -ock-nant*
Llanrhidian	*thlann-ridd-yann*
Llanrug	*thlann-reeg*
Llanrwst	*thlann-roost*
Llansadwrn	*thlann-sadd-ooern*
Llansanffraid	*thlann-sann-fried*
Llansannan	*thlann-sannann*
Llansantffraid- Cwmteuddwr	*thlann-sant-fried- -koomm-tay-thooer*
Llansawel	*thlann-sow-ell* ("sow" rhymes with "now")
Llantarnam	*thlann-tarn-amm*
*Llanthony	*lann-tonny*
Llantrisant	*thlann-trissant*
*Llantwit	*lann-twitt*
Llantysilio	*thlann-tuss-ill-yo*
Llanuwchllyn	*thlann-yook-thlinn*
Llanwddin	*thlann-oothe-inn*
Llanwern	*thlann-wairn*
Llanwnda	*thlann-oonn-dah* ("ah" as in "ah!")

Llanwnog	*thlann-oonnogg*
Llanwrda	*thlann-ooer-dah* ("ah" as in "ah!")
Llanwrtyd	*thlann-ooer-tidd*
Llanybydder	*thlann-a-buthair* ("u" as in "but")
Llanybyther	*thlann-a-buthair* ("u" as in "but")
Llanycil	*thlann-a-kill*
Llanymynech	*thlann-a-munneck*
Llanystumdwy	*thlann-a-stimm-dooey*
Llareggub	*thlar-eggubb*
Llaregyb	*thlar-eggibb*
Llawhaden	*thlow-haddenn* ("thlow" rhymes with "now")
Llechwedd	*thleck-weth*
*Lleyn	*lain*
Llithfaen	*thlith-vine*
Llugwy	*thligg-ooey*
Llwyngwril	*thlooinn-goorrill*
Llwyn-onn	*thlooinn-onn*
Llwynypia	*thlooinn-a-peeah* ("ah" as in "ah!")
Llyn Alaw	*thlinn allow*
Llyn Brenig	*thlinn brennigg*
Llyn Brianne	*thlinn bree-annay*
Llyn Celyn	*thlinn kellinn*
Llyn Cerrig Bach	*thlinn kerrigg bahk* ("ah" as in "ah!")
Llyn Idwal	*thlinn idd-wal* (rhymes with "pal")
Llyn Llydaw	*thlinn thluddow* (rhymes with "now")
Llyn Ogwen	*thlinn ogg-wenn*
Llyn Padarn	*thlinn paddarn*
Llysnewydd	*thleess-naywith*
Llyswen	*thleess-wenn*
Llywernog	*thloe-air-nogg*
Machen	*mackenn*
Machynlleth	*mack-unth-leth*
Maelienydd	*mile-yennith*
Maenclochog	*mine-klockogg*
Maentwrog	*mine-toorrogg*
Maerdy	*mire-dee*
Maesteg	*mice-taig*
Maesyronnen	*mice-a-ronnenn*
Malltraeth	*math-trye-th*
Mallwyd	*math-looidd*

Manafon	*mann-avvonn*
***Manorbier**	*mannor-beer*
Marchlyn	*mark-linn*
Margam	*mar-gamm*
Mathafarn	*math-avvarn*
Mathrafal	*math-ravval* (rhymes with "pal")
Mawddach	*mouthe-ack*
Meifod	*may-vodd*
Meirionnydd	*may-ree-onnith*
Mellte	*meth-tay*
Menai	*menn-eye*
Merthyr	*mair-theer*
Migneint	*migg-naint*
Minera	*minn-errah* ("ah" as in "ah!")
Minffordd	*minn-forthe*
Mochdre	*mock-dray*
Moel Famau	*moil vamm-ah*
Moelfre	*moil-vray*
Moel Hebog	*moil hebbogg*
Moel Siabod	*moil shabbodd*
Morfa Bychan	*morvah buckann* ("ah" as in "ah!")
Morfa Dinlle	*morvah dinn-thlay* ("ah" as in "ah!")
Morfa Nefyn	*morvah nevvinn* ("ah" as in "ah!")
Mostyn	*moss-tinn*
Mwnt	*moont*
Myddfai	*muth-vye* ("uth" as "oth" in "other")
Mynachlog Ddu	*munn-ack-logg thee*
Mynydd Eppynt	*munnith eppint*
Mynydd Hiraethog	*munnith heer-eye-thogg*
Nanhoron	*nann-horronn*
Nanmor	*nann-mor*
Nanteos	*nant-ayoss*
Nant Ffrancon	*nant frann-konn*
Nant Gwernol	*nant gwair-noll*
Nant Gwrtheyrn	*nant gooer-thairn*
Nant Peris	*nant perriss*
Nant-y-glo	*nant-a-glo*
Nant yr Eira	*nant-a-rairah* ("ah" as in "ah!")
Narberth	*nar-bairth*
***Neath**	*neeth*

Nefyn	*nevvinn*
*Nevern	*nevvun*
Ogwr	*oggooer*
Pandy Tudur	*pann-dy tiddeer*
Pant-glas	*pant-glahss* ("ah" as in "ah!")
Pantperthog	*pant-pair-thogg*
Pantrhiwgoch	*pant-roo-gauk*
Pantycelyn	*pant-a-kellinn*
Parys	*parriss*
*Pembroke	*pemm-bruck*
Penarth	*penn-arth*
Penbontbren	*penn-bont-brenn*
Pen-bont-	*penn-bont-*
Rhydybeddau	*-reed-a-beth-eye*
Pencader	*penn-kaddair*
Pen-clawdd	*penn-clowthe* (rhymes with "mouthe")
Penderyn	*penn-derrinn*
Penegoes	*penn-eggoiss*
Pengelli Fach	*penn-gethly vahk* ("ah" as in "ah!")
Penglais	*penn-glice*
Penisa'r-waun	*penn-issar-wine*
Penmachno	*penn-mack-no*
Penmaen-mawr	*penn-mine-mowr* (rhymes with "hour")
Pennant Melangell	*pennant mell-ang-eth*
Penparcau	*penn-park-eye*
Penrhiw-ceibr	*penn-roo-kaibair*
Penrhyndeudraeth	*penn-rinn-day-drye-th*
Pentre-Dolau-Honddu	*penn-tray-doll-eye-honn-thee*
Pentrefelin	*penn-trevv-ellin*
Pentrefoelas	*penn-trevv-oilass*
Pentre Ifan	*penn-tray ivvann*
Pentrwyn	*penn-trooinn*
Pentwyn	*penn-tooinn*
Pen-y-bont	*penn-a-bont*
Pen-y-bryn	*penn-a-brinn*
Penyclawdd	*penn-a-clowthe* (rhymes with "mouthe")
Pen-y-darren	*penn-a-darrenn*

Pen y Fan	*penn-a-vann*
Pen-y-groes	*penn-a-groiss*
Pili Palas	*pilly palace*
Pistyll Rhaeadr	*pistith rye-addar*
Plasnewydd	*plahss-naywith* ("ah" as in "ah!")
Plas y Brenin	*plahss-a-brenninn* ("ah" as in "ah!")
Plas yn Rhiw	*plahss unn roo* ("ah" as in "ah!")
Plwmp	*ploomp*
*Plynlimon	*plinn-limmunn*
Pontardawe	*pont-ar-dow-ay* ("dow" rhymes with "now")
Pontarddulais	*pont-ar-thill-ice*
Pontcanna	*pont-kannah*
Pontcysyllte	*pont-kuss-uth-tay*
Pont-dôl-goch	*pont-doll-gauk*
Ponterwyd	*pont-erroo-idd*
Pontrhydfendigaid	*pont-reed-venn-diggide* (rhymes with "side")
Pont Rhydgaled	*pont-reed-galledd* ("gall" as in "galley")
Pont-rhyd-y-groes	*pont-reed-a-groiss*
Pontsticill	*pont-stickith*
Pontyberem	*pont-a-berremm*
Pont-y-Pair	*pont-a-pyre*
*Pontypool	*pont-a-pool*
Pontypridd	*pont-a-preethe*
Porth-cawl	*porth-cowl*
Porthdinllaen	*porth-dinn-thline*
Porthmadog	*porth-maddogg*
Porth Mawr	*porth mowr* (rhymes with "hour")
Porth Neigwl	*porth-naigool*
Powys	*powiss* ("pow" rhymes with "now")
Preseli	*press-elly*
Prestatyn	*press-tattinn*
Pumsaint	*pimm-sign-t*
Pwll-du	*pooth-dee*
Pwllheli	*pooth-helly*
*Raglan	*ragg-lunn*
Rhandir-mwyn	*rann-deer-mooinn*
*Rhayader	*rye-adder*
Rheidol	*ray-doll*

Rhinog Fach	*rinnogg vahk* ("ah" as in "ah!")
Rhinog Fawr	*rinnogg vowr* (rhymes with "hour")
Rhiwlas	*roo-lass*
Rhondda	*ronn-thah* ("ah" as in "ah!")
Rhoscolyn	*ross-kollinn*
Rhosili	*ross-illy*
Rhosllannerchrugog	*ross-thannair-kriggogg*
Rhosneigr	*ross-naigeer*
Rhostryfan	*ross-truvvann*
Rhuddlan	*rith-lann*
Rhydcymerau	*reed-kumm-air-eye*
Rhydfelen	*reed-vellenn*
Rhydyronnen	*reed-a-ronnenn*
Rhyl	*rill*
***Rhymney**	*rumney*
Rhoshirwaun	*ross-hear-wine*
***Ruabon**	*roo-abbon*
***St Donats**	*saint donnats*
Seiont	*say-ont*
Senghennydd	*seng-hennith*
Sgethrog	*sketh-rogg*
Sgwd yr Eira	*skood a rairah* ("ah" as in "ah!")
Sirhywi	*sear-howee* ("how" rhymes with "now")
Sycharth	*suckarth*
Sychnant	*suck-nant*
Sygyn	*sugg-inn*
Tafolwern	*tavvoll-wairn*
Talerddig	*tal-air-thigg* ("tal" rhymes with "pal")
Talgarth	*tal-garth* ("tal" rhymes with "pal")
Talsarnau	*tal-sarn-eye* ("tal" rhymes with "pal)
Tal-y-bont	*tal-a-bont* ("tal" rhymes with "pal")
Tal-y-llyn	*tal-a-thlinn* ("tal" rhymes with "pal")
Tal-y-sarn	*tal-a-sarn* ("tal" rhymes with "pal")
Tanat	*tannatt*
Tan-y-bwlch	*tann-a-boolk*
Tan-y-graig	*tann-a-grye-g* ("grye-g" rhymes with "tig-(er)")
Tanygrisiau	*tann-a-grish-eye*
Tawe	*tow-ay* ("tow" rhymes with "now")
Teifi	*tavy*

*Tenby	*tenn-by*
Tirabad	*teer-abbadd*
Tongwynlais	*tonn-gwinn-lice*
Tonyrefail	*tonn-a-revvile* (rhymes with "smile")
Tonypandy	*tonn-a-pandy*
Torfaen	*tor-vine*
Torpantau	*tor-pant-eye*
Traeth Bach	*trye-th bahk* ("ah" as in "ah!")
Traethgwyn	*trye-th-gwinn*
Traeth Mawr	*trye-th mowr* (rhymes with "hour")
Traeth y De	*trye-th a day*
Traeth y Gogledd	*trye-th a gogg-leth*
Trawsfynydd	*trowss-vunnith* ("trowss" rhymes with "grouse")
Trearddur	*tray-arthe-ear*
Tredegar	*tredd-eggar*
Trefecca	*trevv-eckah* ("ah" as in "ah!")
Trefeglwys	*trevv-egg-lewis*
Trefforest	*treff-orrest*
Trefor	*trevvor*
Trefriw	*trevv-roo*
Trehafod	*tray-havvodd*
Tregaron	*tregg-arronn*
Tremadog	*tremm-addogg*
*Treorchy	*tree-orky*
Tre'r Ceiri	*trair-kairy*
*Tretower	*tree-tower*
Trimsaran	*trimm-sarrann*
Troedrhiwdalar	*troid-roo-dallar* ("dall" as in "dally")
Trwyn Cilan	*trooinn killann*
Tryfan	*truvvann*
Tryweryn	*troe-errinn*
Tudweiliog	*tidd-wail-yogg*
Twrch	*tooerk*
Twymyn	*tooey-minn*
Tycanol	*tee-kannoll*
Tŷ Hyll	*tee hith*
Tŷ Mawr	*tee mowr* (rhymes with "hour")
Tyn-y-groes	*teen-a-groiss*
Tywi	*towy* (rhymes with "snowy")

Tywyn	*toe-in*
Uwchmynydd	*yook-munnith*
Waunfawr	*wine-vowr* (rhymes with "hour")
Wenallt	*wenn-atht*
Wylfa	*ooill-vah* ("ah" as in "ah!")
Ynys Angharad	*unniss-ang-harradd*
Ynys Fach	*unniss-vahk* ("ah" as in "ah!")
Ynys-hir	*unniss-hear*
Ynys-las	*unniss-lahss* ("ah" as in "ah!")
Ynys Lochtyn	*unniss lock-tinn*
Ynysybwl	*unniss-ubbool*
Yr Eifl	*a raivill*
Yr Harbwr	*er har-booer*
Yr Wyddfa	*a rooith-vah* ("ah" as in "ah!")
Ysbyty Ifan	*uss-putty ivvann*
Ysbyty Ystwyth	*uss-putty ust-with* (rhymes with "pith")
Ystalyfera	*uss-tal-a-verrah* ("tal" rhymes with "pal", "ah" as in "ah!")
Ystradfellte	*uss-tradd-veth-tay*
Ystradgynlais	*uss-tradd-gun-lice*
Ystradmeurig	*uss-tradd may-rigg*
Ystradowen	*uss-tradd-owen*
Ystwyth	*uss-tooith*

Suggested pronunciation from page 98:

ystwyth	winding	*uss-tooith*
gwynt	wind	*gwinnt*
newydd	new	*naywith*

Alphabetical List of Place Name Elements

[river] etc. means this word is the name of a river, mountain etc.

= **Garmon** etc. means this is a different form of the same name.

A word about meanings. These don't always come in the same order in Welsh as in English. **Afon** means "river" and **wen** means "white", but **Afonwen** means "white river".

You may also sometimes have to put in the words "of" and "the" to make sense. For example, **pen** means "head", **y** means "the" and **bont** means "bridge", but **Pen-y-bont** means "(The) head (of) the bridge".

aber	river mouth	*abbair*
Aeron	[river]	*eye-ronn*
afon	river	*avvonn*
allt	hillside	*ath-t*
Aman	[river]	*ammann*
Aran	[mountain]	*arrann*
arian	silver	*arry-ann*
Armon	= **Garmon**	*ar-mon*
arw	rough	*arroo*
aur	gold	*ire*
awel	breeze	*ow-ell* ("ow" as in "now")
awelon	breezes	*ow-ellonn* ("ow" as in "now")
bach	small	*bahk* ("ah" as in "ah!")
Badarn	= **Padarn**	*baddarn*
bae	bay	*bye*
ban	peak	*bann*
banc	bank	*bank*
Bangor	[town]	*bang-gor*
bant	valley	*bant*
barc	field	*bark*
bedd	grave	*bathe*
beddau	graves	*beth-eye*

119

Bedr	Peter	*beddair*
Bedrog	= **Pedrog**	*bedd-rogg*
bedw	birches	*beddoo*
bedwen	birch	*bedd-wenn*
beili	yard	*bailey*
ben	end, top	*benn*
bendigaid	blessed	*benn-diggide* (rhymes with "side")
Beris	= **Peris**	*berriss*
berllan	orchard	*bairth-lann*
berth	hedge, bush	*bairth*
betws	oratory	*bettooss*
beudy	cowshed	*baidy*
blaen	summit	*bline*
blaenau	summits	*bline-eye*
blaidd	wolf	*blithe*
blas	mansion	*blahss* ("ah" as in "ah!")
bod	dwelling	*bawd*
boeth	hot	*boith*
boncyn	hillock	*bonn-kinn*
bont	bridge	*bont*
borfa	pasture	*borvah*
brain	crows	*brine*
brân	crow	*brahn* ("ah" as in "ah!")
bre	hill	*bray*
bren	timber	*brenn*
brenin	king	*brenninn*
brith	mottled	*breeth*
bron	slope	*bronn*
brwyn	rushes	*bruin*
bryn	hill	*brinn*
buarth	yard	*bee-arth*
budr	foul	*biddeer*
bugail	shepherd	*biggile* (rhymes with "smile")
bwlch	gap, pass	*boolk*
bwll	pit, pool	*booth*
bwthyn	cottage	*boothinn*

bychan	little	*buckann*
bylchau	gaps, passes	*bulk-eye*
byr	short	*beer*
caban	hut	*kabbann*
cadair	chair	*kaddire* (rhymes with "fire")
Cadfan	[saint]	*kadd-vann*
cae	field	*kye*
caer	fort	*kyre*
caled	hard	*kalledd*
cam	crooked	*kamm*
canol	middle	*kannoll*
cantref	district	*kann-trevv*
capel	chapel	*kappell*
carn	cairn	*karn*
carnedd	cairn	*karneth*
carreg	stone	*karregg*
carrog	torrent	*karrogg*
cartre	home	*kar-tray*
cartref	home	*kar-trevv*
castell	castle	*kass-teth*
cawr	giant	*kowr* (rhymes with "hour")
cefn	ridge	*kevvenn*
cegin	kitchen	*kegginn*
cei	quay	*kay*
ceiliog	cock	*kail-yogg*
Ceiriog	[river]	*kay-ree-ogg*
Celert	[saint]	*kellairt*
celli	grove	*kethly*
celyn	holly trees	*kellinn*
celynnen	holly tree	*kell-unnenn*
Cemais	[town]	*kemm-ice*
cennin	leeks	*kenninn*
cerrig	stones	*kerrigg*
cewri	giants	*kayoo-ry*
cil	corner	*kill*
cist	coffer	*kist*
clafdy	hospital	*klavv-dy*

clawdd	dyke, ditch	*klowthe* (rhymes with "mouthe")
clwyd	hurdle	*klooidd*
clyd	sheltered	*kleed*
Clywedog	[river]	*kloe-eddogg* ("kloe" rhymes with "hoe")
coch	red	*kawk*
coed	trees, wood	*koid*
coety	house in wood	*koity*
cog	cuckoo	*kaug*
collen	hazel tree	*koth-lenn*
com(m)ins	common	*komm-ince*
Conwy	[river,town]	*konn-ooey*
corn	horn	*korn*
cors	bog	*korss*
Cothi	[river]	*kothy*
craig	rock	*krye-g*
crib	ridge	*kreeb*
cribin	ridge	*kribbinn*
crin	withered	*krinn*
croes	cross (road)	*kroiss*
crug	hillock	*kreeg*
crwn	round	*kroon*
Curig	[saint]	*kirrigg*
cwm	valley	*koomm*
cwrt	court	*kooert*
Cybi	[saint]	*kubby*
cyll	hazel trees	*kith*
cymer	confluence	*kummair*
Cyfeiliog	[river]	*kuvv-ail-yogg*
Cynon	[river]	*kunnonn*
cyrn	horns	*keern*
Dafydd	David	*davvith*
dan	under	*dann*
dau	two	*die*
Dawe	= Tawe	*dow-ay* ("dow" rhymes with "now")
dawel	calm	*dow-ell* ("dow" rhymes with "now")
ddau	two	*thy*

dderw	oaks	*therroo*
dderwen	oak	*thair-wenn*
ddeu	two	*they*
Ddewi	= **Dewi**	*they-wy*
ddinas	fort, city	*thinnass*
ddu	black	*thee*
ddŵr	water	*thooer*
ddwy	two	*thooey*
de	south	*day*
deg	fair	*daig*
Deilo	= **Teilo**	*dailo*
derw	oaks	*derroo*
derwen	oak	*dair-wenn*
deu	two	*day*
Dewi	David	*day-wy*
din	fort	*dinn*
dinas	fort, city	*dinnass*
dir	land	*deer*
diserth	wilderness	*dissairth*
dôl	meadow	*dole*
dolau	meadows	*doll-eye*
domen	mound	*dommenn*
don	wave	*donn*
draen	thorn	*drine*
draeth	beach	*drye-th*
drain	thorns	*drine*
dre	town	*dray*
dref	town	*drave*
dri	three	*dree*
drindod	trinity	*drinn-dodd*
drum	ridge	*drimm*
du	black	*dee*
Dudno	= **Tudno**	*did-know*
Dulais	[river]	*dill-ice*
Dulas	[river]	*dill-ass*
dŵr	water	*dooer*
dwy	two	*dooey*
dŷ	house	*dee*
dyffryn	valley	*duff-rinn*
Dyfi	Dovey	*duvvy*

Dyfnant	[river]	*duvv-nant*
Dyfrdwy	Dee	*duvver-dooey*
dyrys	difficult	*durriss*
Dysilio	= **Tysilio**	*duss-ill-yo*
dywyll	dark	*doe-ith* ("doe" rhymes with "hoe")
Edw	[river]	*eddoo*
efail	smithy	*evvile* (rhymes with "smile")
eglwys	church	*egg-lewis*
eifl	forked peak	*aivill*
Einion	[person]	*ain-yonn*
Einon	[person]	*ainonn*
eira	snow	*airah* ("ah" rhymes with "ah!")
eithin	gorse	*aithinn*
Elan	[river]	*ellann*
Emlyn	[person]	*emm-linn*
Emrys	[person]	*emm-riss*
eos	nightingale	*ayoss*
erw	acre	*erroo*
eryr	eagle	*erreer*
esgair	ridge	*ess-kire* (rhymes with "fire")
fach	small	*vahk* ("ah" rhymes with "ah!")
faen	stone	*vine*
faer	steward	*vyre*
faes	field	*vice*
Fair	Mary	*vyre*
Faldwyn	= **Maldwyn**	*vall-dooinn*
fan	peak, place	*vann*
fawnog	peat-bog	*vow-nogg* ("vow" rhymes with "now")
fawr	big	*vowr* (rhymes with "hour")
fechan	little	*veckann*
fedw	birches	*veddoo*
fedwen	birch	*vedd-wenn*
Fellte	= **Mellte**	*veth-tay*
felen	yellow	*vellenn*
felin	mill	*vellinn*
felys	sweet	*velliss*
fendigaid	blessed	*venn-diggide* (rhymes with "side")
fer	short	*vair*
ffin	boundary	*finn*
ffordd	road	*forth*
ffos	ditch	*fauss*

ffridd	pasture, alp	*freethe* (rhymes with "breathe")
ffrwd	stream	*frood*
ffynnon	well	*funnonn*
Fihangel	Michael	*veehang-ell*
foel	bare hilltop	*voil*
fôr	sea	*vor*
forwyn	maiden	*vor-winn*
fraith	mottled	*vrye-th*
frân	crow	*vrahn* ("ah" as in "ah! ")
fre	hill	*vray*
fron	slope	*vronn*
fryn	hill	*vrinn*
fudr	foul	*viddeer*
fynydd	mountain	*vunnith*
gadair	chair	*gaddire* (rhymes with "fire")
Gadfan	= Cadfan	*gadd-vann*
gaer	fort	*ghyre* ("gh" as in "ghetto")
galed	hard	*galledd*
gallt	hill	*gath-t*
gam	crooked	*gamm*
ganol	middle	*gannoll*
Garmon	[saint]	*gar-monn*
garn	cairn	*garn*
garreg	stone	*garregg*
garrog	torrent	*garrogg*
garth	enclosure	*garth*
gartre	home	*gar-tray*
gartref	home	*gar-trevv*
garw	rough	*garroo*
gawres	giantess	*gow-ress* ("gow" rhymes with "now")
gefn	ridge	*gevvenn* ("g" as in "get")
gegin	kitchen	*gegginn* ("g" as in "get")
geiliog	cock	*gail-yogg*
Gelert	= Celert	*gellairt* ("g" as in "get")
gelli	grove	*gethly* ("g" as in "get")
gelyn	holly trees	*gellinn* ("g" as in "get")
gelynen	holly tree	*gell-unnenn* ("g" as in "get")
glan	bank, shore	*glann*
glas	blue	*glahss* ("ah" as in "ah!")
gloddfa	quarry	*gloth-vah* ("ah" as in "ah!")
glyd	sheltered	*gleed*

glyn	valley	*glinn*
goch	red	*gauk*
goed	trees, wood	*goed*
goetre	house in wood	*goy-tray*
gof	smith	*gauv*
gog	cuckoo	*gaug*
gogledd	north	*gogg-leth*
gollen	hazel tree	*goth-lenn*
gors	bog	*gorss*
graig	rock	*grye-g*
gribin	ridge	*gribbinn*
grisiau	steps	*grish-eye*
groes	cross	*groiss*
grug	hillock,heather	*greeg*
Gurig	= **Curig**	*girrigg* ("g" as in "give")
gwalch	hawk	*gwalc* ("alc" rhymes with "talc")
gwaun	moor	*gwine*
gwen	white, fair	*gwenn*
gwern	swamp	*gwairn*
gwig	wood	*gweeg*
gwm	valley	*goomm*
gwrt	court	*goort*
Gwy	Wye	*gwee*
Gwyddel	Irishman	*gwithell*
gwyn	white, fair	*gwinn*
gwynt	wind	*gwint*
Gybi	= **Cybi**	*gubby*
gyll	hazel trees	*gith* ("g" as in "give")
Gynolwyn	[river]	*gunn-oll-winn*
Gynon	= **Cynon**	*gunnonn*
gyrn	horns	*geern* ("g" as in "get")
Hafesp	[river]	*havvesp*
hafod	summer home	*havvodd*
hafoty	summer home	*havvotty*
Hafren	Severn	*havv-renn*
haul	sun	*hile*
hebog	hawk	*hebbogg*
heli	salt water	*helly*
helyg	willows	*helligg*
hen	old	*hane*
hendra	winter home	*henn-drah* ("ah" as in "ah!")
hendre	winter home	*henn-dray*

126

hendref	winter home	*henn-drevv*
heol	road	*hayoll*
Hepste	[river]	*hepp-stay*
heulog	sunny	*hailogg*
hir	long	*here*
Hopcyn	Hopkin	*hopkin*
hyfryd	pleasant	*huvv-ridd*
Hywel	[king]	*how-ell*
iarth	yard	*yarth*
Idris	[person]	*idd-riss*
Idwal	[person]	*idd-wal* (rhymes with "pal")
Iestyn	[person]	*yess-tinn*
Ifan	John	*ivvann*
is	lower	*eess*
isa	lowest	*issah*
isaf	lowest	*issavv*
Ithon	[river]	*ith-onn*
laeth	milk	*lye-th*
lan	church, shore	*lann*
las	blue	*lahss* ("ah" as in "ah!")
le	place	*lay*
lech	slate	*lake*
llaeth	milk	*thlye-th*
llan	church	*thlann*
llannerch	glade	*thlann-airk*
llawr	ground	*thlowr* (rhymes with "hour")
lle	place	*thlay*
llech	slate	*thlake*
llechwedd	slope	*thleck-weth*
llethr	slope	*thleth-air*
lluest	cabin	*thlee-est*
llwyd	grey	*thlooidd*
llwyn	grove, bush	*thlooinn*
llydan	wide	*thluddann*
llyn	lake	*thlinn*
llys	court	*thleess*
Llywelyn	[prince]	*thloe-ellinn*
lwyd	grey	*looidd*
lwyn	bush	*looinn*
lydan	wide	*luddann*
lyn	lake, valley	*linn*
lys	court	*leess*

127

Madog	[person]	*maddogg*
maen	stone	*mine*
maer	steward	*mire*
maes	field	*mice*
Mair	Mary	*mire*
Maldwyn	Baldwin	*mall-dooinn* ("all" as in "alley")
march	horse	*mark*
marchog	knight	*mark-ogg*
mawnog	peat-bog	*mow-nogg* ("mow" rhymes with "now")
mawr	big	*mowr* (rhymes with "hour")
meirch	horses	*mairk*
Meirion	[person]	*may-ree-onn*
Melangell	[person]	*mell-ang-eth*
melin	mill	*mellinn*
Mellte	[river]	*meth-tay*
melyn	yellow	*mellinn*
melys	sweet	*melliss*
merthyr	martyr	*mair-theer*
Mihangel	Michael	*mee-hang-ell*
min	edge	*minn*
moch	pigs	*mauk*
moel	bare hilltop	*moil*
môr	sea	*mor*
morfa	marsh	*mor-vah* ("ah" as in "ah!")
morwyn	maiden	*mor-winn*
mur	wall	*meer*
mwyn	mild, ore	*mooinn*
mynydd	mountain	*munnith*
Myrddin	[person]	*mer-thinn*
nant	brook	*nant*
neuadd	hall	*nayath*
newydd	new	*naywith*
nos	night	*nauss*
oer	cold	*oir*
ogof	cave	*oggovv*
on, onn	ash trees	*onn*
onnen	ash tree	*onnenn*
Padarn	[saint]	*paddarn*
pant	valley	*pant*
parc	field	*park*
Pedr	Peter	*peddair*
Pedrog	[saint]	*pedrogg*

128

pen	top	*penn*
penarth	headland	*penn-arth*
pennau	tops, ends	*penn-eye*
penrhyn	headland	*penn-rinn*
pentre	village	*penn-tray*
pentref	village	*penn-trevv*
Peris	[saint]	*perriss*
perllan	orchard	*pairth-lann*
perth	hedge, bush	*pairth*
pistyll	waterfall	*pistith*
plas	mansion	*plahss* ("ah" as in "ah!")
plwyf	parish	*plooivv*
poeth	hot	*poith*
poncyn	hillock	*ponn-kinn*
pont	bridge	*pont*
porfa	pasture	*por-vah* ("ah" as in "ah!")
porth	harbour	*porth*
Powys	[kingdom]	*powiss* ("pow" rhymes with "now")
pren	timber	*prenn*
pridd	soil	*preethe*
pum	five	*pimm*
pump	five	*pimp*
pwll	pit, pool	*pooth*
'r	the	*'r*
rhaeadr	waterfall	*rye-addar*
rhandir	allotment	*rann-deer*
rhedyn	bracken	*reddinn*
Rheidol	[river]	*ray-doll*
rhiw	slope	*roo*
rhos	moor	*rauss*
rhyd	ford	*reed*
riw	slope	*roo*
rug	heather	*reeg*
ryd	ford	*reed*
Sadwrn	Saturn	*sadd-ooern*
Saeson	Englishmen	*sigh-sonn* ("sonn" rhymes with "gone")
saint	saints	*sign-t*
sant	saint	*sant*
sarn	causeway	*sarn*
scwd	waterfall	*skood*
Siencyn	Jenkin	*shenn-kinn*

Soch	[river]	*sauk*
sticill	stile	*stickith*
sych	dry	*seek*
tai	houses	*tie*
tair	three	*tyre*
tal	end	*tal* (rhymes with "pal")
tan	under	*tann*
Tanat	[river]	*tannatt*
Tawe	[river]	*toway* ("tow" rhymes with "now")
tawel	calm	*towell* ("tow" rhymes with "now")
teg	fair	*taig*
Tegid	[lake]	*teggidd*
Teilo	[saint]	*tailo*
tir	land	*teer*
tocyn	small heap	*tockinn*
tomen	mound	*tommenn*
ton	waste land	*tonn*
traeth	beach	*trye-th*
traws	across	*trowss* (rhymes with "grouse")
tre	town	*tray*
tref	town	*trave*
tri	three	*tree*
trindod	trinity	*trinn-dodd*
trwyn	promontory	*trooinn*
Tudno	[saint]	*tidd-no*
twlc	pigsty	*toolk*
twr	tower	*tooer*
Twrch	[river]	*tooerk*
Twrog	[person]	*toorrogg*
tŷ	house	*tee*
tyddyn	small farm	*tuthinn* ("uth" as "oth" in "other")
tŷn	small farm	*teen*
Tysilio	[saint]	*tuss-ill-yo*
tywyll	dark	*towith* ("tow" rhymes with "low")
ucha	highest	*ickah*
uchaf	highest	*ickavv*
uwch	higher	*yook*
waun	moor	*wine*
wen	white, fair	*wenn*
wern	swamp	*wairn*
wig	wood	*weeg*

Wrw	[person]	*oorroo*
Wy	Wye	*we*
wyddfa	tomb	*ooith-vah* ("ah" as in "ah!")
wyn	white, fair	*winn*
wynt	wind	*wint*
Wysg	Usk	*ooisk*
y	the	*uh* (or "a" as in "a book")
ym	in	*umm*
yn	in	*unn*
ynys	island	*unniss*
yr	the	*urr*
ysbyty	hospital	*uss-putty*
ysgawen	elder tree	*uss-kowenn* ("kow" sounds like "cow")
ysgubor	barn	*uss-kibbor*
ystrad	vale	*uss-tradd*
ystum	bend in river	*uss-timm*
ystwyth	winding	*uss-tooith*

Alphabetical List of People's Names

Including characters from history and old tales as well as names given to Welsh children today. The middle column shows the matching English name, or if there isn't one, it shows "[f]" for "female" or "[m]" for "male", together with the meaning if known.

Aled	[m]	*alledd*
Alis	Alice	*alliss*
Alun	Alan	*allinn*
Alwyn	[m]	*al-winn* ("al" rhymes with "pal")
Alys	Alice	*alliss*
Amlyn	[m]	*amm-linn*
Aneirin	[m]	*ann-airinn*
Aneurin	[m]	*ann-airinn*
Angharad	[f]	*ang-harradd*
Anwen	[f]	*ann-wenn*
Arawn	[m]	*arrown* (rhymes with "gown")
Arfon	[m]	*ar-vonn*
Arianrhod	Silver Wheel [f]	*arry-ann-rodd*
Arianwen	Silver White [f]	*arry-ann-wenn*
Arwel	[m]	*ar-well*
Arwyn	[m]	*ar-winn*
Bendigeidfran	Blessed Bran [m]	*bendy-gaid-vrann*
Bethan	Beth	*bethann* ("beth-" rhymes with "breath")
Beti	Betty	*betty*
Betsan	Betsy	*bett-sann*
Beuno	[m]	*baino*
Bevan	[surname]	*bevvann*
Bevin	[surname]	*bevvinn*
Bleddyn	[m]	*bleth-inn* ("bleth-" rhymes with "breath")
Blodeuwedd	Flower Form [f]	*blodd-ay-weth*
Blodwen	White Flower [f]	*blodd-wenn*
Brân	Crow [m]	*brahn* ("ah" as in "ah!")
Branwen	White Crow [f]	*brann-wenn*

Bronwen	White Breast [f]	*bronn-wenn*
Bryn	Hill [m]	*brinn*
Brynach	[m]	*brunnack*
Buddug*	Victoria	*bithigg* ("bith-" rhymes with "with")
Cadfael	[m]	*kadd-vile*
Cadfan	[m]	*kadd-vann*
Cadwaladr	[m]	*kadd-walladar* ("all" as in "alley")
Cai	[m]	*kye*
Caradoc	[m]	*karradd-ock*
Caradog	[m]	*karradd-ogg*
Carwyn	[m]	*kar-winn*
Caryl	Carol	*karrill*
Carys	[f]	*karriss*
Catrin	Catherine	*katt-rinn*
Ceinwen	Fine White [f]	*kain-wenn*
Celert	[m]	*kellairt*
Cen	Ken	*kenn*
Cennard	[m]	*kennard*
Ceri	[m]	*kerry*
Ceridwen	[f]	*kerridd-wenn*
Ceryl	Carol	*kerrill*
Cerys	[f]	*kerriss*
Cigfa	[f]	*kigg-vah* ("ah" as in "ah!")
Cledwyn	[m]	*kledd-winn*
Clwyd	[surname]	*klooidd*
Culhwch	[m]	*kill-hook*
Cunedda	[m]	*kinn-eth-ah*-ah
Cybi	[m]	*kubby*
Cyngen	[m]	*kung-enn*
Cynan	[m]	*kunnann*
Cynog	[m]	*kunnogg*
Dafis	[surname]	*davviss*

***Buddug** is the Welsh form of Boudica (Boadicea), the Queen of the Iceni who fought against the Romans. Her name means "Victorious" - the wrong name for her, as it turned out.

Dafydd	David	*davvith*
Dai	Dave	*dye*
Dei	Dave	*day*
Deilwen	White Leaf [f]	*dail-wenn*
Deiniol	[m]	*dain-yoll*
Deio	Davey	*dayo*
Delyth	[f]	*dellith*
Dewi	David	*day-wy*
Dic	Dick	*dick*
Dilys	[f]	*dilliss*
Dwynwen	[f]	*dooinn-wenn*
Dyfrig	[m]	*dove-rigg*
Dyfyr	[m]	*duvveer*
Dylan	[m]	*dullann*
Edmwnd	Edmund	*edd-moond*
Efnisien	[m]	*evv-nishenn*
Eiddwen	[f]	*aithe-wenn*
Eifion	[m]	*aiv-yonn*
Eigra	[f]	*aigrah* ("ah" as in "ah!")
Einir	[f]	*aineer*
Eira	Snow[f]	*ai-rah* ("ah" as in "ah!")
Eirian	[m]	*ay-ree-ann*
Eirwen	[f]	*air-wenn*
Eirlys	[f]	*air-liss*
Eirys	[f]	*ai-riss*
Elen	Ellen	*ellenn*
Eleri	[f]	*ell-erry*
Elfed	[m]	*ell-vedd*
Elfyn	[m]	*ell-vinn*
Elin	Ellen	*ellinn*
Elinor	Eleanor	*ell-innor*
Elis	Ellis	*elliss*
Eliseg	[m]	*ell-issegg*
Eluned	[f]	*ell-innedd*
Elwyn	[m]	*ell-winn*
Emlyn	[m]	*emm-linn*
Emrys	Ambrose	*emm-riss*
Emyr	[m]	*emmeer*

Endaf	[m]	*enn-davv*
Enfys	Rainbow [f]	*enn-viss*
Eryl	[f]	*errill*
Esyllt	Isolda	*essith-t*
Eurgain	Fine Gold [f]	*airg-ine*
Eurig	[m]	*ai-rigg*
Euros	[m]	*ai-ross*
Eurwen	White Gold [f]	*air-wenn*
Euryn	[m]	*ai-rinn*
Evan	John	*evvann*
Evans	[surname]	*evvanz*
Falmai	[f]	*vall-mye*
Falyri	Valerie	*valerie*
Ffion	Fiona	*fee-onn*
Fflur	Flora	*fleer*
Ffowc	Ffoulkes	*fouk*
Ffransis	Francis	*francis*
Ffred	Fred	*fred*
Gaenor	Gaynor	*guy-nor*
Gareth	[m]	*garreth*
Garmon	[m]	*gar-monn*
Geraint	[m]	*gerr-ine-t* ("g" as in "get")
Gerallt	Gerald	*gerrath-t* ("g" as in "get")
Gethin	[m]	*gethinn* ("geth" rhymes with "breath", "g" as in "get")
Gilfaethwy	[m]	*ghyll-vye-thooey*
Glan	Shore[m]	*glann*
Glanmor	Seashore[m]	*glann-mor*
Glenys	[f]	*glenniss*
Glyn	Glen	*glinn*
Glyndwr	Water Glen [m]	*glinn-dooer*
Goronwy	[m]	*gorr-onn-ooey*
Gronw Befr	[m]	*gronnoo bevvair*
Gruffudd	[m]	*griffith*
Gruffydd	[m]	*griffith*
Grug	Heather	*greeg*
Gryffudd	[m]	*griffith*
Guto	Guy	*gitto* ("g" as in "get")

Gwawl	[m]	*gwowl* (rhymes with "howl")
Gwawr	Dawn	*gwowr* (rhymes with "hour")
Gwen	White [f]	*gwenn*
Gwenallt	White Hill [m]	*gwennath-t*
Gwenan	Little White [f]	*gwennann*
Gwenfil	[f]	*gwenn-vill*
Gwenllian	[f]	*gwenn-thleeann*
Gwennan	Little White [f]	*gwennann*
Gwenno	Whitey [f]	*gwenno*
Gwenwynwyn	[m]	*gwenn-winn-winn*
Gwerfyl	[f]	*gwair-vill*
Gwern	[m]	*gwairn*
Gwilym	William	*gwillimm*
Gwion	[m]	*gweeonn*
Gwri Wallt Euryn?	Fair Hair [m]	*goorry wath tay-rinn*
		("wath" rhymes with "path")
Gwrtheyrn	[m]	*gooer-thairn*
Gwydion	[m]	*gwidd-yonn*
Gwyn	White [m]	*gwinn*
Gwyneth	[f]	*gwinneth*
Gwynfor	White Sea [m]	*gwinn-vor*
Gwynn	White [m]	*gwinn*
Gwynne	White [m]	*gwinn*
Haf	Summer [f]	*halve*
Hafgan	Summer Song [f]	*havv-gann*
Hafina	Summer [f]	*havv-innah* ("ah" as in "ah!")
Hafwen	White Summer [f]	*havv-wenn*
Harri	Henry/Harry	*harry*
Hefin	[m]	*hevvinn*
Heledd	[f]	*helleth*
Heulwen	Sunshine [f]	*hail-wenn*
Hiraethog	Yearning [m]	*heer-eye-thogg*
Huw	Hugh	*hugh*
Huws	Hughes	*hugh-ss*
Hyfaidd Hen	[m]	*huvv-eye-th hain*
Hywel	[m]	*how-ell*

Hywel Dda	Hywel the Good [m]	*how-ell thah* ("ah" as in "ah!")
Idris	[m]	*idd-riss*
Idwal	[m]	*idd-wal* (rhymes with "pal")
Iestyn	Justin	*yess-tinn*
Ieuan	John	*yea-ann*
Ifan	John	*ivvann*
Ifans	Evans	*ivvann-ss*
Ifanwy	[f]	*ivv-ann-ooey*
Illtud	[m]	*ith-tidd*
Illtyd	[m]	*ith-tidd*
Indeg	[f]	*inn-degg*
Ioan	John	*yo-ann*
Iola	[f]	*yollah* ("ah" as in "ah!")
Iolo	[m]	*yollo*
Iolo Goch	Ginger Iolo [m]	*yollo gawk*
Iolo Morganwg	Glamorgan Iolo [m]	*yollo mor-gannoogg*
Iorwerth	[m]	*yor-wairth*
Islwyn	[m]	*iss-looinn*
Ithel	[m]	*ith-ell*
Iwan	John	*ee-wann*
Jac	Jack	*jack*
Jaci	Jackie	*jackie*
Lhuyd	Lloyd	*thlooidd*
Lili	Lily	*lily*
Llefelys	Pleasant Place [m]	*thlevv-elliss*
Lleu Llaw Gyffes	[m]	*thlay thlow guffess*
Llew	Leo [m]	*thlayoo*
Llifon	[m]	*thlivvonn*
Llinos	Linnet [f]	*thlinnoss*
Lloyd	Grey	*loid*
Lludd	[m]	*thleethe*
Llwyd	Grey	*thlooidd*
Llyr	[m]	*thleer*
Llywelyn	[m]	*thloe-ellinn*
Lowri	Laurie/Laura	*lowry*
Luned	[f]	*linnedd*
Mabon	[m]	*mabbonn*

Macsen Wledig Emperor Maximus *maxenn leddigg*
Madog [m] *maddogg*
Maelgwn Hound Prince [m] *mile-goon*
Magi Maggie *maggie*
Mai May *mye*
Mair Mary *mire*
Mallt [f] *math-t*
Manawydan [m] *mannow-uddann* ("ow" rhymes with "now")
Manon [f] *mannonn*
Mared [m] *marraid*
Maredudd [m] *marreddith*
Marged Margaret *marg-edd*
Margiad Margaret *marg-yadd*
Mari Mary *marry*
Maryl [f] *marrill*
Math [m] *math*
Matholwch [m] *math-ollook*
Mathonwy [m] *math-onn-ooey*
Medi Harvest [f] *meddy*
Megan [f] *meggann*
Meilyr [m] *maileer*
Meinir [f] *maineer*
Meirion [m] *may-ree-onn*
Meleri [f] *mell-erry*
Melfyn Melvyn *mell-vinn*
Menna [f] *mennah* ("ah" as in "ah!")
Meredydd [m] *merreddith*
Mererid Margaret/Pearl *merrerridd*
Merfyn Mervyn *mair-vinn*
Merfyn Frych Spotty Mervyn [m] *mair-vinn vreek*
Meri Mary *mary*
Meurig [m] *may-rigg*
Mihangel Michael *meehang-ell*
Moelwyn [m] *moil-winn*
Moi [m] *moy*
Morfudd [f] *mor-vith*
Morgan [m] *mor-gann*
Morus Maurice/Morris *morriss*

Morys	Maurice/Morris	*morriss*
Mostyn	[m]	*moss-tinn*
Myfanwy	[f]	*muvv-annooey*
Myrddin	[m]	*mer-thinn*
Nans	Nancy	*nance*
Nansi	Nancy	*nancy*
Nerys	[f]	*nerriss*
Nesta	[f]	*ness-tah* ("ah" as in "ah!")
Nia	[f]	*nee-ah* ("ah" as in "ah!")
Nisien	[m]	*nishenn*
Non	[f]	*naun*
Ogwen	[m]	*ogg-wenn*
Olwen	[f]	*oll-wenn*
Osian	[m]	*osh-ann*
Owain	[m]	*ow-ine*
Owain Lawgoch	Owain Redhand [m]	*ow-ine low-gauk*
		("low" rhymes with "now")
Owen	[m]	*owen*
Padarn	[m]	*paddarn*
Pedr	Peter	*peddair*
Pedrog	[m]	*pedd-rogg*
Peredur	[m]	*perreddeer*
Pryderi	[m]	*prudd-erry*
Prys	Son of Rhys	*preess*
Puw	Son of Huw	*pew*
Pwyll	[m]	*pooith*
Rees	[surname]	*reess*
Rheinallt	Reginald	*rain-ath-t*
Rhian	Queen [f]	*ree-ann*
Rhiannon	Great Queen [f]	*ree-annonn*
Rhigyfarch	[m]	*rigg-uvvark*
Rhidian	[m]	*ridd-yann*
Rhisiart	Richard	*rishart*
Rhodri	Roderick	*rodd-ry*
Rhodri Mawr	Rhodri the Great	*rodd-ry mowr* (rhymes with "hour")
Rhonabwy	[m]	*ronn-abb-ooey*
Rhosier	Roger	*roshair*

Rhydderch	[m]	*ruddairk*
Rhys	[m]	*reess*
Robat	Robert	*robbatt*
Sali	Sally	*sally*
Sara	Sarah	*sah-rah* ("ah" as in "ah!", both times)
Shân	Jane	*shahn* ("ah" as in "ah!")
Sian	Jane	*shahn* ("ah" as in "ah!")
Sieffre	Geoffrey	*sheff-ray*
Siencin	Jenkin	*shenn-kinn*
Siôn	John	*shaun*
Sioned	Janet	*shonnedd*
Siwan	Jane	*shoo-ann*
Siwsann	Susan	*sue-sann*
Stifyn	Stephen	*steevinn*
Sulwen	Whitsun [f]	*sill-wenn*
Sulwyn	Whitsun [m]	*sill-winn*
Talfan	[m]	*tal-vann* ("tal" rhymes with "pal")
Taliesin	[m]	*tally-essinn*
Tegwen	Fair White [f]	*tegg-wenn*
Teifryn	[m]	*tay-vrinn*
Teilo	[m]	*tailo*
Terfel	[surname]	*tair-vell*
Tewdwr	Lord of the People	*tue-dooer*
Teyrnon	Great King	*tair-nonn*
Tomos	Thomas	*tommoss*
Trebor	[m]	*trebbor*
Trefor	[m]	*trevvor*
Tudno	[m]	*tidd-no*
Tudur	Lord of the People	*tiddeer*
Twm	Tom	*toomm*
Watcyn	Watkin	*watkin*
Wyn	White [m]	*winn*
Wynn	White [m]	*winn*
Wynne	White [m]	*winn*

Alphabetical List of Pub Names

The alphabetical order in this list ignores the words "y" and "yr", both meaning "the".

Afon Goch	Red River	*avvonn gauk*
Afon Teifi	River Teifi	*avvonn tavy*
Yr Allweddau Croes	The Cross Keys	*a rath-weth-eye kroiss*
Y Bedol	The Horseshoe	*a beddoll*
Brynffynnon	Spring Hill	*brinn-funnonn*
Y Cadno a'r Cwn	The Fox and Hounds	*a kadd-no ar koonn*
Cadwgan	Cadugan	*kadd-ooggann*
Cae'r Bedol	Horseshoe Field	*kyre beddoll*
Caia	Fields	*kye-a* ("ah" as in "ah!")
Y Ceffyl Du	The Black Horse	*a keffill dee*
Cefn Glas	Green Ridge	*kevvenn glahss* ("ah" as in "ah!")
Cegin Arthur	Arthur's Kitchen	*kegginn artheer*
Cerdinen	Hawthorn	*kair-dinnenn*
Cerrigllwydion	Grey Stones	*kerrigg-thlooidd-yonn*
Clwb y Bont	Bridge Club	*kloobb a bont*
Clwb Brynmenyn	Butterhill Club	*kloobb brinn-menninn*
Clwb Ifor Bach	Little Ivor Club	*kloobb ivvor bahk* ("ah" as in "ah!")
Cymro	Welshman	*kumm-ro*
Y Dafarn Goch	The Red Inn	*a davvarn gauk*
Y Dafarn Newydd	The New Inn	*a davvarn naywith*
Y Ddraig Goch	The Red Dragon	*a thrye-g gauk*
Y Delyn	The Harp	*a dellinn*
Derwen	Oak Tree	*dair-wenn*
Yr Enfys	The Rainbow	*a renn-viss*
Ffwrwm Ishta	Sitting Bench	*foorroomm ish-tah* ("ah" as in "ah!")
Y Ffynnon Arian	The Silver Spring	*a funnonn arry-ann*
Gardd Fôn	The Garden of Anglesey	*garth vaun*
Y Gegin Fawr	The Big Kitchen	*a gegginn vowr* (rhymes with "hour")
Gloch Las	Blue Bell	*glauk lahss* ("ah" as in "ah!")
Glyn y Weddw	The Widow's Glen	*glinn a weth-oo*
Y Goron	The Crown	*a gorronn*
Gwarcefel	?	*gwar-kevvell*

Y Gwesty Bach	The Little Inn	*a gwess-ty bahk* ("ah" as in "ah!")
Gwesty'r Oen	The Lamb Inn	*gwess-ty roin*
Gwindy	Winehouse	*gwinn-dy*
Y Gwter Fawr	The Big Gutter	*a goottair vowr* (rhymes with "hour")
Hen Dafarn y Polyn	The Old Pole Inn	*hain davvarn a pollinn*
Yr Hen Dŷ	The Old House	*ur hain dee*
Hywel Dda	Howell the Good	*howell thah* ("ah" as in "ah!")
Ifor Hael	Ivor the Generous	*ivvor hyle*
Llannerch	Glade	*thlannairk*
Y Llety	The Inn	*a thletty*
Llety Lloegr	The England Inn	*thletty thloigeer*
Y Llew Coch	The Red Lion	*a thlew kauk*
Y Llong	The Ship	*a thlong*
Llwyncelyn	Holly Bush	*thlooinn-kellinn*
Llwyn Dafydd	David's Bush	*thlooinn davvith*
Maelgwn	[Welsh king]	*mile-goonn*
Maes y Gwaed	The Field of Blood	*mice a gwide*
Maesllwch	The Field of Dust	*mice-thlook*
Owain Glyndŵr	[Welsh hero]	*ow-ine glinn-dooer*
Pant-yr-Ardd	The Garden Hollow	*pant-a-rarth*
Y Pedwar Ci	The Four Dogs	*a pedd-war kee*
Pen-y-Bont	The End of the Bridge	*penn-a-bont*
Pen-y-bryn	The Top of the Hill	*penn-a-brinn*
Pen-dref	The End of the Town	*penn-drave*
Penlan Fawr	The Big Church End	*penn-lann vowr* (rhymes with "hour")
Penlan Oleu	The Bright Church End	*penn-lann ollay*
Penllwyndy	The Bush End House	*penn-thlooinn-dy*
Pen Nionyn	Onion Head	*penn-nee-onninn*
Penpompren	The End of the Wooden Bridge	*penn-pomm-prenn*
Penrhiwgaled	The Top of the Steep Hill	*penn-rew-galledd*
Penrhiwllan	The Top of Church Hill	*penn-rew-thlann*
Y Pentan	The Hearth	*a penn-tann*
Y Pentre	The Village	*a penn-tray*
Penylan	The Church End	*penn-a-lann*
Pontygwindy	The Winehouse Bridge	*pont-a-gwinn-dy*
Rhiwderin	Bird Hill	*rew-derrinn*
Rhos yr Hafod	The Summer House Marsh	*rauss-ur-havvodd*

Rhyd y Blew	The Ford of the Hairs	*reed-a-blew*
Y Sgwar	The Square	*a squar* (rhymes with "far")
Tafarn yr Aradr	The Plough Inn	*tavvarn a rarra-dar*
Tafarnaubach	Little Inns	*tavv-arn-eye-bahk* ("ah" as in "ah!")
Tafarn Bach	Little Inn	*tavvarn bahk* ("ah" as in "ah!")
Tafarn y Bachgen Du	The Black Boy Inn	*tavvarn a bahk-genn dee* ("ah" as in "ah!")
Tafarn y Bont	The Bridge Inn	*tavvarn a bont*
Tafarn-bwlch	Inn of the Pass	*tavvarn-boolk*
Tafarn y Cadno a'r Helgwn	The Fox and Hounds Inn	*tavvarn a kadd-no ar hell-goonn*
Tafarn y Crydd	The Cobbler's Inn	*tavvarn a kreethe*
Tafarn Cwm Owen	The Owen Valley Inn	*tavvarn koomm owen*
Tafarn y Dyffryn	The Valley Inn	*tavvarn a duff-rinn*
Tafarn y Felin	The Mill Inn	*tavvarn a vellinn*
Tafarn y Fic	The Vic Inn	*tavvarn a vick*
Tafarn-y-Garreg	The Rock Inn	*tavvarn-a-garregg*
Tafarn-y-Gath	The Cat Inn	*tavvarn-a-gahth* ("ah" as in "ah!")
Tafarn Gelyn	Holly Inn	*tavvarn gellinn* ("g" as in "get")
Tafarn Glan yr Afon	The River Bank Inn	*tavvarn glann a ravvonn*
Tafarn y Gof	The Smith's Inn	*tavvarn a gauv*
Tafarn Gors Bach	The Little Bog Inn	*tavvarn gorse bahk* ("ah" as in "ah!")
Tafarn y Grisiau	The Steps Inn	*tavvarn a grish-eye*
Tafarn y Groes	The Cross Inn	*tavvarn a groiss*
Tafarn y Milgi	The Greyhound Inn	*tavvarn a milg-y*
Tafarn-y-Mynach	The Monk Inn	*tavvarn-a-munnack*
Tafarn-y-Mynydd	The Mountain Inn	*tavvarn-a-munnith*
Tafarn y Parciau Bach	The Little Fields Inn	*tavvarn a parky-eye bahk* ("ah" as in "ah!")
Tafarn Pen Gors	The Bog End Inn	*tavvarn penn gorse*
Tafarn Pen Rhiw	The Hill Top Inn	*tavvarn penn rew*
Tafarn y Plu	The Feathers Inn	*tavvarn a plee*
Tafarn y Rhos	The Moor Inn	*tavvarn a rauss*
Tafarn y Rhwyth	?	*tavvarn a rooith*
Tafarn y Rhyd	The Ford Inn	*tavvarn a reed*

Tafarn y Sosban	The Saucepan Inn	*tavvarn a soss-pann*
Tafarn Tŷ Coch	The Red House Inn	*tavvarn tee kauk*
Tafarn y Werin	The Folk Inn	*tavvarn a werrinn*
Tafarnyfedw	The Birches Inn	*tavvarn-a-veddoo*
Troedrhiwfuwch	The Bottom of Cow Hill	*troid-rew-vewk*
Tu-hwnt-i'r-Afon	Over the River	*tee-hoont-ear-avvonn*
Tŷ Gwyn	White House	*tee gwinn*
Y Tŷ Gwyrdd	The Green House	*a tee gweerth*
Tŷ Fry	High House	*tee vree*
Tŷ Isaf	Bottom House	*tee issavv*
Ty'n y Capel	Chapel House	*teen a kappell*
Ty'n Coed	Wood House	*teen koid*
Tŷ Newydd	New House	*tee nay-with*
Ty'n Llan	Church House	*teen thlann*
Ty'n-y-Mynydd	Mountain House	*teen a munnith*
Ty'n Porth	Gate House	*teen porth*
Tŷ Tawe	Tawe House	*tee toway* ("tow" rhymes with "now")
Tŷ Uchaf	Top House	*tee ickavv*
Wern	Marsh	*wairn*

144